Printed by CreateSpace
4900 LaCross Road
North Charleston, South Carolina 29406

Cover Illustrations:
Cover, Sunday Record-Herald, "Lady Liberty and Liberty Bell," New
York Public Library, Public Domain collection;
Backcover, Trumplosion Image, ParentRap, Pixabay image.

For interior illustration credits, see pages 277-282, which function as an
extension of this page.

Library of Congress Control Number 2017911899

ISBN   978-0-9992471-0-5 PCN/loc paperback
          978-0-9992471-1-2 Kindle (Mobi)
          978-0-9992471-2-9 iBooks (ePub)

Published by Trumplosion LLC

Hybrid publication: poetry, non-fiction, and fiction. United States—
Political Commentary. United States—Social Life.

Dear Reader,

When things happen in my life, I write about them. Writing gives me a way to unpack and explore my feelings about things, events, and people. I teach reading and writing, so I often show my writing to my students as examples of what writing can do to help people unclutter and understand their thoughts and feelings. Since writing is a method for me to sort through conflict, emotional confusion, and depression, I write on a number of topics that I need to explore.

What you hold in your hand is a series of poems, essays, and short stories that I have written over the past year or more in trying to come to terms with the extraordinary 2016 presidential campaign and then the election of Donald J. Trump as the 45th president of the United States of America—something that I see as a national and global travesty. The items are grouped by "pre-election" and "post-election," but the "post-election" items have been further grouped by genre: all the poetry together, then essays, and then the short stories (which are fictional stories based our present situation). So the "post-election" items are not presented chronologically. For example, after Trump's negative and inaccurate Tweets about John Lewis on

January 14, 2017, I initially tried to write a poem about the situation, but my thoughts wouldn't be contained in a poem and morphed into "A Vindication of John Lewis." However, I come back John Lewis in the poem, "Inauguration Day," because of Trump's opaque reference to Lewis in his speech on January 20th.

When I have shared these writings with individuals whom I know, the responses have been positive. Trump's base, however, is stubbornly supportive, maybe because, the effects of what he has done thus far, have not yet been felt. Many of the people I know are truly horrified and alarmed by the state of the nation, and they have found my writing perhaps not comforting but expressive of the outrage and frustration they feel. Because it is my sense that so many of us feel such frustration and outrage about current events, I offer these items to a wider audience with the hope they help to give expression to the feelings that others share with me. I hope they inspire others to write and create other expressions the outrage and frustration we feel. Dissent is patriotic, and the First Amendment gives us the right of freedom of expression which includes protesting.

Lastly, I realize that there is a significant amount of repetition in these collected items (poems, essays, and short stories). Please indulge me and take the subtitle of *Trumplosion* to heart *Writing as a Coping Mechanism*. Trump, as a candidate and as president, continually came/comes back to outrageous and divisive topics and themes that I didn't know how to react to but that I felt I had to explore so that I could fully come to terms with them. Each item is an attempt to cope with the tragedy and malignancy of our present situation. Thus, perhaps, you might forgive the repetition and look at each item as an individual expression instead of a methodically planned collection that addresses single issues and moves, start to finish, with less repetition.

PS—Ideally, most of the images for the illustrations in *Trumplosion* would be color images. Due to cost considerations, all of those color images have been converted to black and white illustrations, but some of the vibrance and impact of the images has been lost in this compromise. Perhaps some day in the future, a color edition will be possilbe.

Contents

"When power leads [human beings] toward arrogance, poetry reminds [them] of [their] limitations. When power narrows the area of [human] concerns, poetry reminds [them] of the richness and diversity of existence. When power corrupts, poetry cleanses."
    --John F. Kennedy

"Since the beginning of our American history we have been engaged in change, in a perpetual, peaceful revolution, a revolution which goes on steadily, quietly, adjusting itself to changing conditions without the concentration camp or the quicklime in the ditch. The world order which we seek is the cooperation of free countries, working together in a friendly, civilized society. This nation has placed its destiny in the hands and heads and hearts of its millions of free men and women, and its faith in freedom under the guidance of God. Freedom means the supremacy of human rights everywhere. Our support goes to those who struggle to gain those rights and keep them. Our strength is our unity of purpose."
--Franklin D. Roosevelt

"Here in these United States, where there can be no economic or technical excuse for it, poverty is not only a private tragedy but, a public crime. It is above all a challenge to our morality."
--A. Philip Randolph

"The supreme quality for leadership is unquestionably integrity. Without it, no real success is possible, no matter whether it is on a section gang, a football field, in an army, or in an office."
       --Dwight D. Eisenhower

"Accuracy is the twin brother of honesty; inaccuracy, of dishonesty."
       --Nathaniel Hawthorne

"Honesty, integrity, and accountability, the values which should be the hallmark of this government, have instead been thrown under the bus by an arrogant majority, casualties in a misguided campaign to shield from accountability those who abuse this House."
　　　　--Louise Slaughter

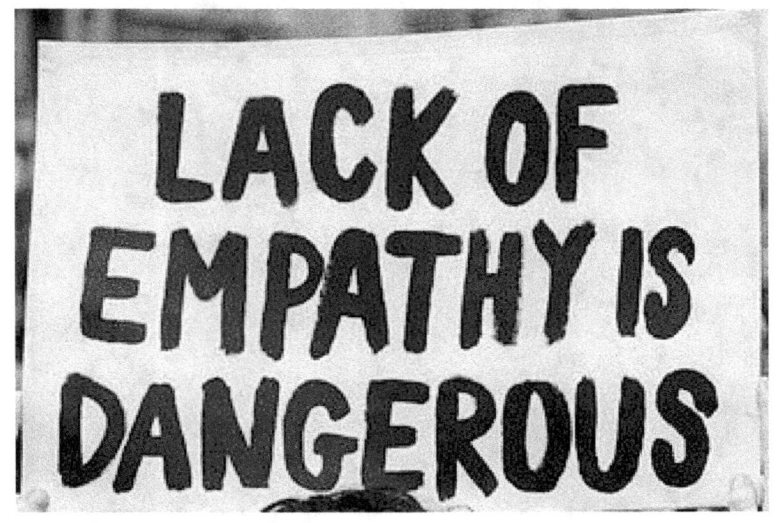

"Men [and women] of integrity, by their very existence, rekindle the belief that as a people we can live above the level of moral squalor. We need that belief; a cynical community is a corrupt community."
　　　　--John W. Gardner

"No other candidate for the White House this year has anything close to Trump's record of repeated social and business dealings with mobsters, swindlers, and other crooks.... From the public record and published accounts ... it's possible to assemble a clear picture of what we do know. The picture shows that Trump's career has benefited from a decades-long and largely successful effort to limit and deflect law enforcement investigations into his dealing with top mobsters, organized crime associates, labor fixers, corrupt union leaders, con artists and even a one-time drug trafficker whom Trump retained as the head of his personal helicopter service."
  --David C. Johnson

"Trump's entire business career reeks, beginning with his early associations with organized crime and proceeding through a career of swindling.... Trump is not merely comfortable doing business with criminals and thugs—his habit of manipulating bankruptcy laws and swindling his partners have left him reliant upon, let us say, unconventional sources of investment, many of whom are the scum of the earth."
  --Jonathan Chait

"The breadth of Trump's controversies is truly [huge], ranging from allegations of mafia ties to unscrupulous business dealings, and from racial discrimination to alleged marital rape. They stretch over more than four decades, from the mid-1970s to the present day. To catalogue the full sweep of allegations would require thousands of words and lump together the trivial with the truly scandalous."
    --David A. Graham

"Trump in many ways represents the culmination of the deep state. He's a plutocrat who's used the laws, such as business bankruptcy procedures, for his own gain and yet in a way he is frightening people in the deep state because he is so far out, that he's upsetting their business model. The standard model is for billionaires to dictate the candidates' positions on free trade, austerity etc. On the upside: He is scaring the daylights out of members of the deep state. On the downside: He's moving away from the current model of corporate oligarchy with a façade of free elections. Instead, he's using all the populist themes developed by the Republican Party in the past to keep their base happy, but he's actually making promises to act on them and moving towards out-and-out fascism."
    --Mike Lofgren

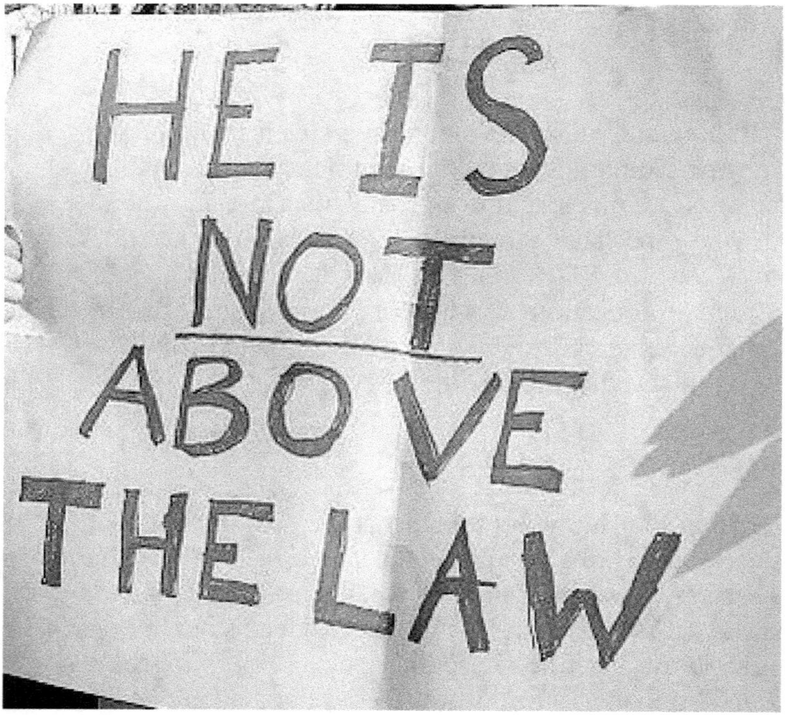
HE IS
NOT
ABOVE
THE LAW

"What will it be like to live, for the next four years, under the rule of a reality TV huckster who boasts nonstop about his so-called achievements, who calls the press his enemy and has promised to shut down and silence dissent?"
   --Jennifer Weiner

"So we lock our doors, and turn our backs, and ignore those in pain and in need. We discriminate against immigrants on the basis of their religion. We look at foreigners with fear. We take away free, accessible birth control. We have found ourselves in some 'Black Mirror' version of 'I Love the '80s,' only with Twitter instead of the tabloids, pussy bows instead of shoulder pads and Ivanka instead of Ivana."
   --Jennifer Weiner

Pre-Election

Poetry

"America Comes First"?

"America Comes First"—
Is that so Important?
And when is the last time
our policies made it look like
We really Cared for more than
Ourselves?

What about Humanity First?
Long ago, Marcus Aurelius told us
Human beings were our Business.
Has that really Changed?
Like it or not,
We're All in this Together,
All of us.
Beyond National Borders,
because there's nowhere else to go.

One Planet, One Future!
We'll take the Animals with us—
to Heaven or Hell.
We must get beyond America First—

because we've been there too long.

Humanity needs to Trump America for
(the) U.S. to be truly Great.

—not Manifest Destiny,
but the most Humane Legacy—
a Legacy for all of us,
not just the Red, White, and Blue.

Wanting to Cry (Friday September 23, 2016)

As I listened to the news today, I wanted to cry.

Little Gabby Hill-Carter's murderer was caught at a

relative's house in Tennessee

—a long way from Camden,

where Tyhan Brown's bullet hit Gabby in the head,

the little eight year old girl had been riding her bike outside

her house,

when she was hit.

The child's death justly galvanized the community

—but what about Tyhan Brown?

He's eighteen,

so young to have his life thrown away.

At what point did Tyhan's bright childhood future

turn down a dark dark path that would lead to a gun and a

murder rap.

Did his single mother not read to him enough?

Could she not shield him from the violence of the streets

and the poverty of the neighborhood?

Was the murder of his father the start of it all?

16

Did the community fail him through poor schools,

neighborhoods plagued with "deep poverty,"

abandoned houses, drugs, crime, and neighbors demoralized

by unemployment, crime, and a lack of social services?

In the name of justice (#justiceforgabby),

we throw another life away,

creating a double tragedy.

Don't get me wrong,

Gabby deserves justice,

but isn't there some other model that

could promote more than retaliation or revenge?

Aren't we past "an eye for an eye"—a life for a life?

Isn't restorative justice worth a try?

In Charlotte, there's the National Guard and a curfew.

Keith Lamott Scott dead at the hands of the police.

Protests turned into rioting

—a bad situation spiraling worse.

Protestor, Justin Carr, shot in the crowd, and ending up dead

with Rayquan Borum charged for the crime.

In Tulsa, a police officer charged with manslaughter

JUSTICE

in the death of Terence Crutcher.

Is it a step forward?

I don't know.

Will the "Ferguson Effect" make police

"reluctant to engage" with suspects?

Is the drop in "pro-active policing" the reason

for the spike in homicide in major cities across the nation

—at a time when crime in general is significantly down?

And who are the victims of spikes in urban homicides?

Mostly men of color.

Ironic and tragic:

how do we, as a nation, deal with that?

Worse, what happens when good people don't want to be

cops?

What happens then?

And the last straw

was listening to clips of Donald Trump talking about

"One nation ... under one God and under one flag"

—it was "Make America Great Again"—all over again.

The U.S.—answerable only to itself,

because the rights of other nations are not as important as

our own.

The Judeo-Christian God supreme,

because other religions are invalid or tainted by association

with extremists,

as if atrocities haven't been committed in the name

of our God, in our own land and in too many others.

One philosophy or ideology imposed on all,

whether they disagree or not.

The tears welled up

—so much pain, so much rage, so much intolerance.

And none of it will get us anywhere.

That's what made me want to cry.

The retaliation model of justice

doesn't bring healing or forgiveness.

Police awareness training and accountability won't stop

"hot spot" policing

while those hot spots are poor, minority, urban

neighborhoods.

The solutions we seek make us ALL accountable

for ending poverty, renewing our cities, fixing our schools,

and so much more.

Second chances need love, forgiveness, and empathy.

Our Union Forever.

Abe Lincoln called us to show the "better angels of our nature," and a man shot him dead.

Martin Luther King, Jr., said,

"Hate cannot drive out hate: only love can do that,"

and he too was shot dead.

John Lennon said, "Love was the answer,"

and he was gunned down too.

Why is it the disciples of love get murdered

while the disciples of hate get an audience?

Because when the going gets tough,

hate is easy and love is hard,

but that is exactly why love is the only path forward,

toward healing and reconciliation.

That we still can't manage to embrace love

makes me want to cry.

Nothing Funny about It

"Boys will be boys"
and use Locker-Room Humor.

What does that mean?

It means Donald Trump and Brock Turner
are two sides of the same coin.

Girls and women aren't human beings to them.

They're tits and legs, asses and pussies;
they exist to service male "you know whats"
with their "you know wheres"
—whether the women are sentient or consenting or not:
"Grab'em by the pussy"
"F*ck them"
—Never mind inconvenient terms like
Rape and Sexual Assault
—even if you do,
they won't stick in a misogynistic culture
where "a star" can do "anything" he wants to
whether a Stanford swimmer or a real estate tycoon,
because judges worry about
the "severe impact" of prison time on a convicted rapist,

not the impact on the victim (of the deplorable act)
of only giving the criminal six months
out of a possible fourteen years for the crime.

And Trump supporters say,
"All normal men"
Objectify girls and women
—so what the hay?
One goes as far as to say,
"All men look at a pretty girl and say 'Wow'"
Trump talking trash just shows he's "human."
"Boys will be boys,"
Men use Locker-Room Humor
because Men are Pigs
—with these excuses we don't confront blatant sexism,
we enable it and condone it.

But let's back it up,
and look at the words,
"All Men look at a pretty Girl"
—in other words, all men objectify women—
Evaluate them in terms of their "f*ckability quotient."
A woman's worth is in her ability to sexually please a man.

her mind, her heart, her soul—
Not as significant as the f*ckability of her pussy.
Is that really the message we want to be sending out?

Worse, men infantilize women
—categorize them as girls,
Children who don't know their own minds.
Can't you just hear the self-justifying rationalization of sexual assault?
"I f*cked the girl—
but it wasn't rape because
she's *just a girl*."
She said, "No"; she said, "Stop,"
but I wanted to, so she must have too,
so I "moved on" her like a b*tch in heat,
and it's okay because she is *just a girl*
and I'm a star and that's what men do.
For Brock Turner, the girl doesn't even need to be conscious, to be raped and dismissed.
Hard to know what Mr. Trump would do in the circumstances,
but he freely gropes and kisses women wherever he can despite the hindrance of a current wife.

"Boys will be boys";

"Locker-Room Humor"

—don't enable gutter talk!

Call it what it is

indecent, crass, profane, obscene,

vile, rude, hideous, offensive,

lewd, crude, repugnant, vulgar, abusive,

and there's nothing humorous or funny about it.

29

Grand Old Party

Grand Old Party, what have you done?

You've set loose on the country a megalomaniac

who says he's the Only One.

A Reality TV star who spews fear and hate.

His claims of a rigged election and a Clinton-backed media

plot

may bring post-election rebellion.

What then, GOP?

Why aren't you reigning him in?

Why can't you see him as the terrorist within our midst?

The Twitter Troll, supreme, spewing fear and hate?

The true threat within our borders?

Not the immigrant, the media, the Clintons,

or the rational voter who all dare to be repelled

by what he says and does.

If elected,

he wouldn't use the Bully Pulpit as a platform for reform,

he'd be the Bully in the Pulpit.

A Commander-in-Chief who's a Tyrant,
with his fingers on Nukes instead of a big stick.
Because he thinks he's the Only One
to fix America's ills,
to Make America Great Again.
Don't be fooled;
he'll make the USA PATRIOT Act
look progressive
and strip his enemies (of which will be, all
who disagree with his rants filled with fear and hate)
of their Constitutional Rights.
What will we be then, GOP?

An acknowledged Rogue Nation,
lead by a self-proclaimed megalomaniac
—with world nations uniting against us
for their own security
and because of the atrocities
within our borders and abroad.
What then, Grand Old Party?

Undermine him while there's still time,
before he undermines us, the U.S.A.

Reign him in before it's too late,

and the whole country, in chaos, is left asking,

"Grand Old Party, what have you done?"

STATUE OF LIBERTY BY NIGHT, NEW YORK CITY.

33

Post-Election

Poetry

A Trump Presidency

I guess you get what you pay for, so to speak.

And America spoke in 2016!

A megalomaniac for Commander-in-Chief

Shove the LGBT community back in the closet.

Build a Wall to keep the "raping," "drug-dealing,"

"criminal" immigrants out of our "great" country.

Re-instate Stop-and-Frisk because

Getting-Tough-on-Crime

hasn't led to a national incarceration crisis

and Black Lives really don't Matter.

Bring back Trickle-Down-Economics

because, somehow, miraculously,

and against global economic trends,

that will bring manufacturing jobs back to the U.S.

Wake Up America!

You've bought yourselves a charlatan!

And global markets know it more than you.

They know that Trump is irrational and unpredictable,

that he's all smoke and mirrors and brash talk.

Why don't you?

We've put the Bully in the pulpit.

The Twitter Troll in command.

The ranting, lying, insensitive man

who makes fun of the disabled,

treats women like trash,

and threatens his enemies with

jail time or bombs.

Bye, bye, *Roe v. Wade*.

Hello, isolationist and completely self-serving America.

God Help Us All!

Woe to the World

The Americans have chosen a self-proclaimed
megalomaniac.

They're following the extremist right trend
foretold by Brexit,
and foreshadowing Le Pen in France,
Wilders in Holland,
and the Pirate Party in Iceland.

With Trump BBFs with Putin
maybe they can get Kim Jong-un
to join the party
for an unholy alliance
to unhinge democracy
across the globe.

Woe to the World!
Dark days ahead.

Heaven Weeps for Us (Wednesday November 9, 2016)

I awoke to a grim, grey day.

Donald J. Trump is the new president-elect.

A racist, misogynistic, homophobic, narcissistic man
to lead the most powerful nation in the world.

Impulsive and divisive,

he'll slam anyone

who disagrees or challenges him.

John Winthrop once famously said in 1630

that their Puritan colony needed to be

"as a City upon a Hill"

with the eyes of the world looking upon them.

He meant that as an experiment in moral

and righteous living,

they would be an example to the peoples of the world,

a beacon of light in a dark world.

What are we today?

"A City upon a Hill"

seeping a darkness of fear and hate

across the land and across the globe.

That isn't rain out there; they're tears.

Heaven weeps for us and what we've become.

I weep too.

Woe to the World: Take 2

Woe to the world, Trump is come!

Let the U.S., receive her new, Commander-in-Chief.

Let every heart, try not to be revolted at the thought.

And girls and women cover your genitals

so you're not groped by the President.

So you're not groped by the President.

Woe to the earth, the Twitter Troll is come!

Let NAFTA and the Trans-Pacific Partnership be
dismantled.

Disregard the Science of Climate Change

and increase practices that will accelerate it.

Withdrawal from NATO.

America under Trump has no regard for world peace.

American under Trump has no regard for natural resources.

American under Trump has no regard for anyone but itself.

Woe to America, Trump will let sorrow grow.

His promises are hollow, manufacturing jobs are gone,

his policies will only benefit the rich,

the poor and the middle class will get the shaft.

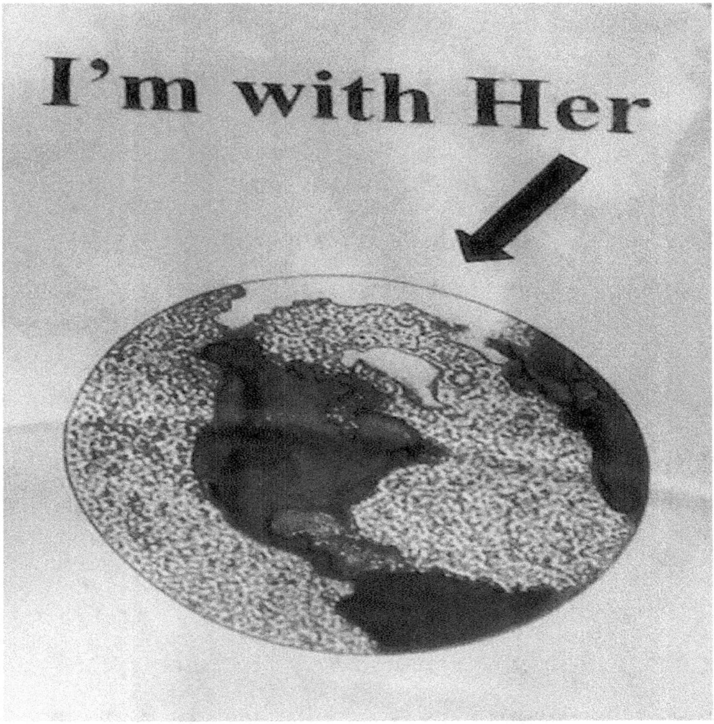
I'm with Her

INTERNATIONAL COOPERATION YEAR 1965
UN
UNITED STATES POSTAGE
5c

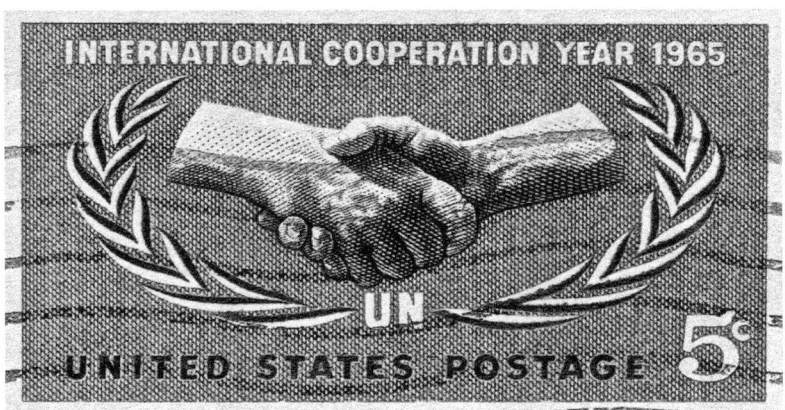

And I guess we deserve it because we voted him in.
And I guess we deserve it because we voted him in.

Woe to America, he leads with fear and hate.
He'll build the Wall to keep Hispanics out.
He'll increase immigrant phobia and restrict who can come in.
He'll take away same-sex marriage and overturn *Roe v. Wade*.
Getting-Tough-on-Crime will hurt the African American community the most, but when enough White kids get locked up,
perhaps Americans will realize they've been played.
Perhaps, then, Americans will realize they've been played.

Once upon a time, it seems,
I looked forward to the yearly Christmas pageant,
and the children singing "Joy to the World,"
but I just can't see it this year.
All I feel is despair.
All I feel is despair.
Woe to the World, Trump is come!

What Did You Expect?

Hey, all you one-issue Trump supporters,

whether you went with him for

Pro-Life, anti-immigrant,

or bringing back manufacturing jobs,

didn't you really look at him,

the whole Trump package?

He's not a nice human being.

He's a racist, bullying, lying, cheating man.

You don't just get the one issue,

you get the whole deal,

and look where that puts us,

with hundreds of cases of hate-fuelled harassment,

intimidation and assaults in the last few days

and the number of hate-crimes growing daily

across the land.

An African American young woman was attacked

at Villanova University Thursday night

by a group of White male students

screaming "Trump!"

The university president denounced

the behavior as "deplorable,"
"not acceptable and not to be tolerated."
And, yet, Villanova is a Catholic university,
so in how many ways did its faculty and its officials
encourage students to vote for Trump
—even if only on the one-issue platform: Pro-Life?
And despite that Pope Francis said that a person
who wanted to build walls without bridges
(aka Trump) wasn't a Christian.
That's right, the head of the Catholic Church
saw past Trump on abortion to find the
Trump's separatist, isolationist, anti-immigrant platform
unChristian.
The Pontiff saw the bigger, nastier Trump picture;
he saw past one issue.

Therein lies our problem.
Trump is not a one issue man.
He made it clear that with him you get the full package,
a package of hate from a
racist, misogynistic, homophobic, narcissistic man
who will encourage those qualities in the nation he governs.
How could you expect anything else?

47

Weren't you paying attention to the things he said
and the extremists attracted to his base?
Didn't you notice he was endorsed by the KKK?
You supported not one, but all of his platforms,
when you voted for him,
the countless ugly and hateful sides of him,
and by doing so, you supported the "basket of deplorables."

Didn't you see the *New York Times* list of
his 282 insulting Tweets?
Trump rarely tried to hide his bad behavior.
Sexual assault—"I can because I'm a star"
—brushed off as "locker-room talk."
Don't count on it.
He bragged that he could shoot someone and not lose voters.
How clearly does he have to say that he's thinks he is above
the law? And why wouldn't his supports think that they,
now, are too?
We have seen his supporters act as hatefully as Trump,
himself
Truly, America, what did you expect?

Can you call election-related harassment and intimidation,
"utterly repugnant,"
"simply deplorable,"
"disgusting behavior,"
when you voted for a man
who can be described in all those ways?
Ugly, hateful, and vile
—that's a significant part of the full Trump package.
How could you really expect that electing a man like that
as Commander-in-Chief
wouldn't embolden people to act like him,
Twitter Troll and self-proclaimed
Sexual Assailant?

The Villanova student
—was she attacked because she was Black
or because she was a woman?
Is she "lucky" she was "just" knocked down
and not dragged somewhere and gang raped?
America, I hope you're revolted by the behavior
inspired by the president-elect.

The UNITED STATES
4c
POSTAGE
I have sworn ...
Hostility against every
form of TYRANNY
over the mind of man
OF AMERICA
Credo

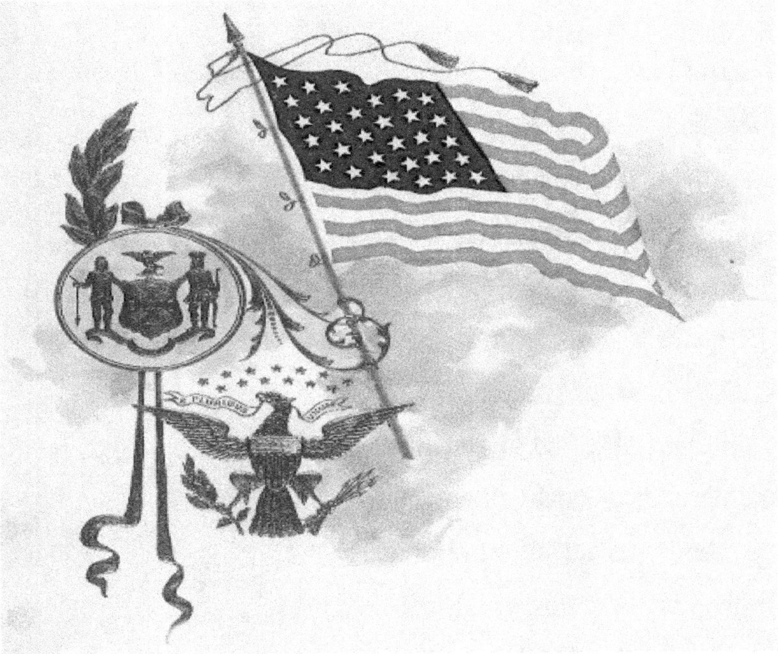

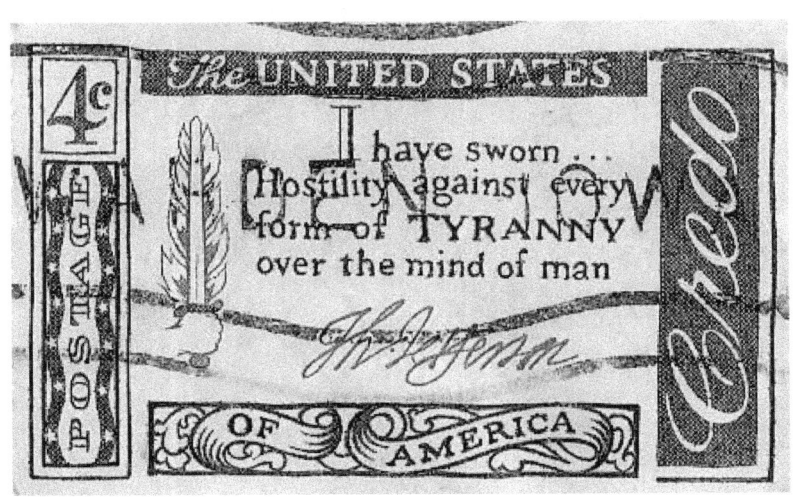

I know I am and more,

sickened and shaken to the core.

Ashamed, utterly and completely ashamed,

in the path Americans have chosen.

Abraham Lincoln asked Americans to rise, show, and act

with their better natures,

their charitable and kinder natures,

the parts of our natures touched by the divine,

"by the better angels of our nature."

In the civil war that confronts us now,

the Trump standard pulls us to our baser natures,

and that is what we are seeing across the land.

How could it not be?

What did you expect?

Trump and His Wives

One important measure of character is
through our relationships.
So what do Trump's wives tell us?
First, they're all former models,
women he dated and married
for their looks and their bodies,
not their minds, achievements
beyond being sex objects,
and/or intellectual and emotional
complexity and passion.
Women who have had who knows how many
cosmetic procedures between them,
because superficial beauty trumps any other for him.

Second, the man marries trophy wives and then "trades up"
when cosmetic procedures aren't enough
or a new "piece of ass" arouses his prick.
(Remember he talks of his own daughter, Ivanka,
as "a nice piece of ass.")
Trump values his wives
for their looks, bust sizes, and

how much pussy they put out.
Trump trading up, like a person might do with cars,
shows how little he honors commitment.
"Till death do us part" is an inconvenient contract
to be weaseled out of just like his business contracts
when they don't suit him.

Melania Trump
has posed naked, of course,
because the "f*ckability quotient"
is what matters to Trump.
There are even "girl-on-girl" pictures,
verging on porn.
Isn't that what every American kid
wants to know about the First Lady
—not her posing in a designer suit
but her birthday suit?

And Americans have elected this man
as Commander-in-Chief,
sending the message that
women are only valuable as sex objects.
Further, he aims to take away women's reproductive rights,

leave them bare-foot and pregnant in their kitchens.

And it might not end there.

When women expressed outrage over the leaked

Access Hollywood tape,

his Twitter Trolls started

#repealthe19th

suggesting that the 19th Amendment,

giving women the right to vote,

should be repealed to help seal up a Trump victory.

Trump and his wives

say a lot about him.

Perhaps not as bad as Henry the Eighth,

but this isn't the 16th Century or an absolute monarchy,

so it's still pretty bad.

A Trump Fascist State

Fascism is an authoritarian and nationalistic
right-wing system of government.

It isn't a democracy because it's led by a dictator,
people's civil rights are restricted,
the press is censored, and the nationalistic agenda
leads to a distorted view of the nation
in terms of its neighboring states and allies.
That can't happen here, people say.

And yet, people said that it couldn't happen in
Germany, Italy, and Argentina.
Hitler, Mussolini, and Peron changed that,
at the cost of millions of lives and endless misery.

Trump is dangerous.
It has been said again and again,
and yet, he's the president-elect.
A charismatic leader (at least to his followers),
the promise to "Make America Great Again,"

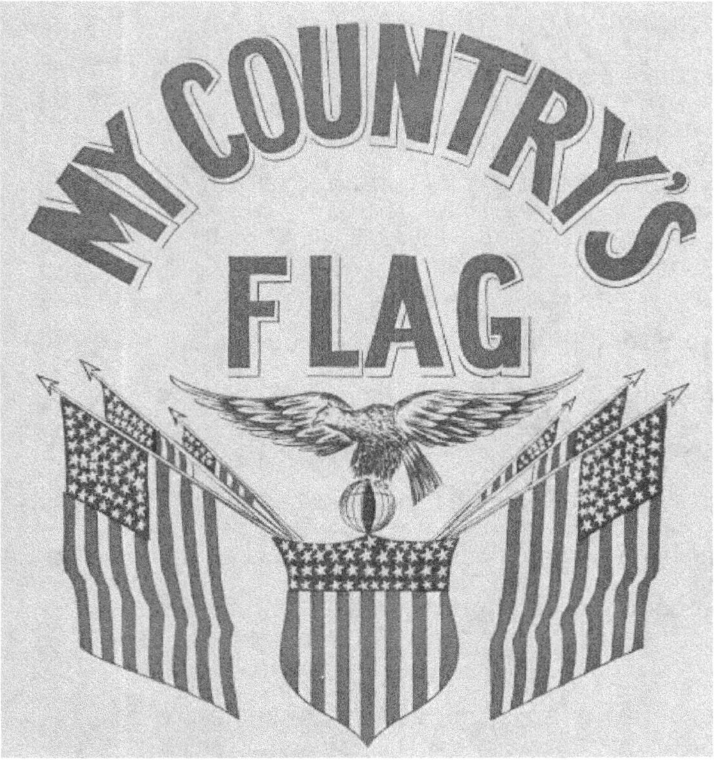
MY COUNTRY'S
FLAG

"OUR REPUBLIC
AND ITS PRESS
WILL RISE OR FALL
TOGETHER"
1847
1947
JOSEPH PULITZER
3¢
UNITED STATES POSTAGE

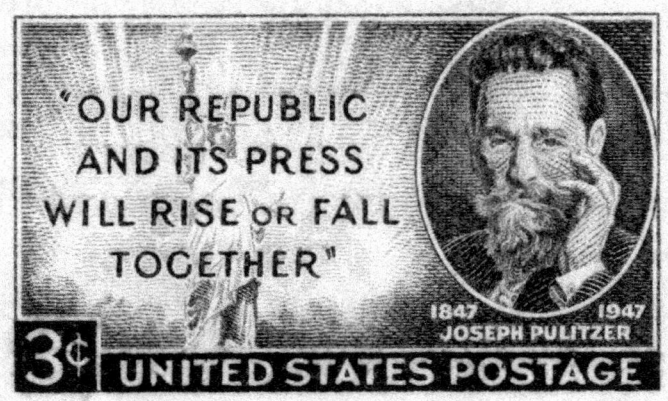

the rhetoric of fear and hate,

the ethnic and racial scapegoats,

the disregard for due process,

the constant chicanery of conspiracy against him

—all the makings of a Trump Fascist State.

His frenzied followers are perpetrating hate-crimes

across the country, venting their rage and frustration

in ways that are, as base and as crass (if not worse),

than their leader, while the famously loud and heedlessly

outspoken Trump stays strangely silent on this civil unrest.

Foreboding what, I am afraid to even imagine.

Violence may be glamorized on TV and in movies,

but real, meaningful solutions to conflict,

aren't resolved through violence.

We resolve issues and heal as human beings,

through empathy, love, tolerance, and forgiveness.

But that doesn't seem to be the Trump way.

In fact, the Trump way points ominously

toward some kind of Fascist State.

AMERICA'S LIGHT FUELED BY TRUTH AND REASON
1.00 USA

Inauguration Day 2017

I didn't think it was supposed to rain today,
but the gravity of the ascension of
Donald J. Trump to the office of the president
of the United States of America
must be too much.
Heaven weeps for us
as it did that grim, grey day
in November when we realized he was
the president-elect.

The Inaugural Address was painful to listen to
lie, after lie, after lie.

Politicians painted as men and women
only interested in enriching themselves
at the expense of common Americans
when it just isn't true.
Some politicians are paid reasonably well,
but nothing like the CEOs and Corporate VPs

making hundreds of millions of dollars
while squeezing every penny out of their workers
and making the decisions to close factories
and terminate jobs when corporate profits fall short
of some formula for the bottom line.

"The people" as "the rulers of the nation again."
Another lie.
That is the whole point of our republic,
there are no rulers, only citizens
and their representatives,
and despite Trump's constant flow of vitriol
and incendiary lies,
most of our elected officials are trying
to do well by their constituencies;
they are in office because they care.

"An education system flush with cash,"
more chicanery.
Tell that to the students and parents in the
School District of Philadelphia,
or in most urban or rural school districts across the country.

DeVos, Trump's pick for the Secretary of Education,
doesn't believe in public schools,
she'll privatize the schools and destroy them,
take a look at the destruction of the
Michigan public schools,
creating even more barriers for the poor
in terms of the American dream.

"America First"—he keeps using that language,
despite it being the name of an isolationist, Anti-Semitic
organization that wanted the U.S. to make concessions
to Hitler during World War II.
Clearly, with Bannon and Sessions at his side,
he doesn't care about racist associations.
And he continues his xenophobia and jingoism
with the audacious statement that
he "will eradicate complete from the face of the Earth"
radical Islamic terrorism
when that is completely beyond anyone's power to promise.
Further, we don't learn from our mistakes.
Operation Desert Shield (1990-1991)
led directly to September 11th, 2001.
What will Operation Iraqi Freedom bring us?

4c
POSTAGE
The UNITED STATES
I have sworn ...
Hostility against every
form of TYRANNY
over the mind of man
OF AMERICA
Credo

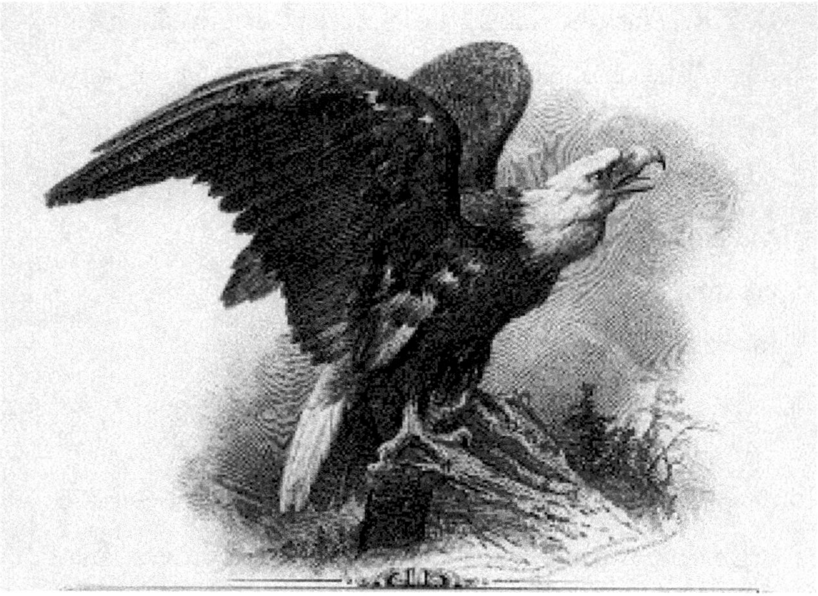

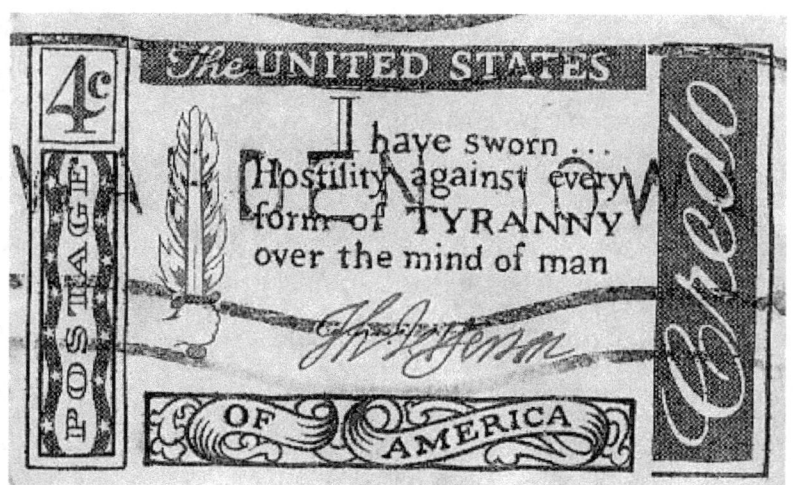

And even if we go to war again over new acts of terrorism,
when will be learn that hate and violence only
breed more hate and violence?

"America will start winning again,"
since when was this a zero-sum game?
We are all in this together,
not just the red and blue,
but the U.S. and all other nations.
We need to fight for world peace, to stabilize the climate,
to reduce poverty at home and abroad,
to end the extremes between the super-rich
(like Trump and his cronies)
and the poor
(who Trump has little intention of helping at all);
they are the "criminals" and "drug dealers" after all.

"The time for talk is over,"
what kind of politician or world leader says that?
We are not on the brink of war.
Yes, actions clearly need to be taken,
but those actions should be carefully
discussed and debated actions; in fact,

the time of talk has just begun.

And insulting a stalwart member of congress (Mr. Lewis),

through a thinly cloaked reference to prior insults,

in one's inaugural address, claiming the desire

for "open," "honest" "debate" and "solidarity,"

is just more Twitter Troll vendetta

against a Civil Rights leader

who would dare to criticize Trump.

Sending the unmistakable message,

that a call for open and honest debate with Mr. Trump

is yet another subterfuge.

Too many Americans are desperate and

deeply unsatisfied,

choosing Trump is clearly reflective of that,

but Trump is a charlatan,

smoke and mirrors,

"sound and fury."

Americans heard what they wanted to hear:

Trump won't be able to do what he promised.

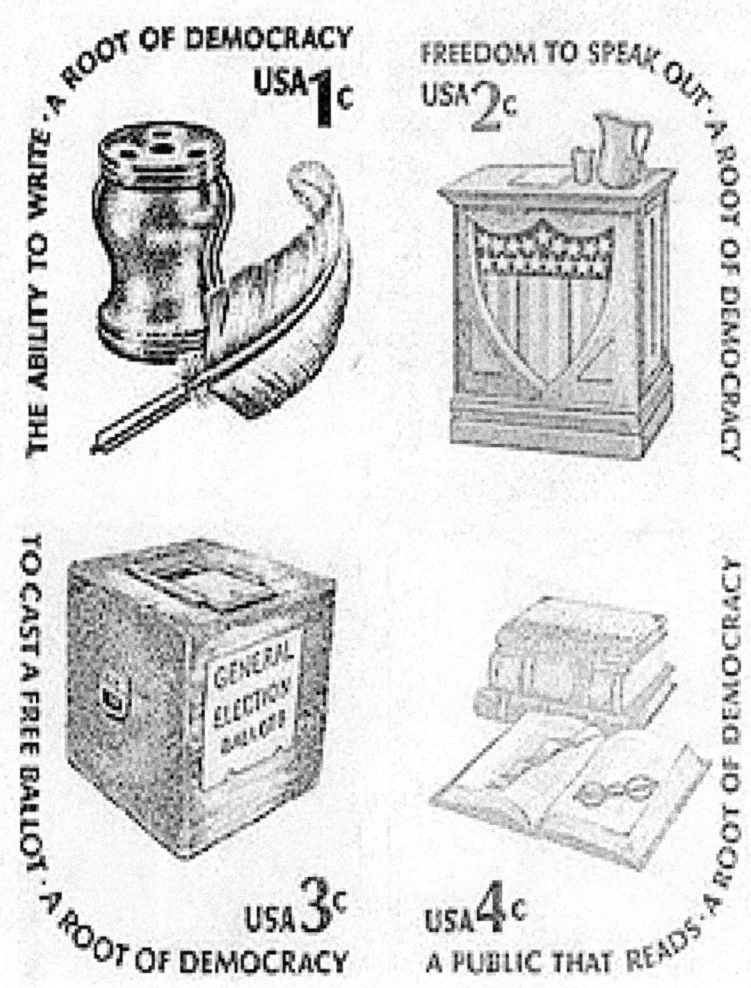

THE ABILITY TO WRITE · A ROOT OF DEMOCRACY
USA 1c

FREEDOM TO SPEAK OUT · A ROOT OF DEMOCRACY
USA 2c

TO CAST A FREE BALLOT · A ROOT OF DEMOCRACY
GENERAL ELECTION BALLOTS
USA 3c

A ROOT OF DEMOCRACY · A PUBLIC THAT READS
USA 4c

Does heaven weep for us,

for Trump's inauguration or as an omen,

for the darkness that lies ahead?

Women's Marches (Saturday January 21, 2017)

Washington, Philadelphia, Chicago, New York, Los
Angeles, Austin, Boston, Minneapolis/St. Paul, Portland,
Seattle, San Francisco, London, Paris, Sydney, Vancouver,
Melbourne, Lisbon, Dublin,
across the United States and across the world
women horrified at the prospect of a
President Donald Trump,
a misogynistic, homophobic, racist, xenophobic,
hateful man, Twitter Troll Supreme, Social Media Bully,
the Bully in the Pulpit.
An aberration, Mr. Trump might say.
Hardly, look at a sampling of what those "nasty women"
and their supporters had to say:

"Pussy Power!"
"Make Canada less appealing again!"
"America's Fascist is not my President!"
"You're Fired! 2020"
"American [Trump image] Horror Story"
"No More Wire Hangers"

72

Family Planning

UNITED STATES 8ᶜ

"Women's Rights are Human Rights"

"F*ck You Orange Hitler"

"My Anger is Justified"

"If Abortion is Murder, then Blowjobs are
    Cannibalism"

"Our bodies, our minds, our power,"

"Refuse to accept a Fascist America"

"Keep your filthy laws off my silky drawers"

"Keep your tiny hands off my rights"

"Girl Power!"

"Nasty woman & proud"

"Vive la resistance, Dump Trump"

"Fight Trump from Abroad"

"Meryl Streep is not overrated, you f*cking piece of
    sh*t"

"Men in tights, for women's rights, stronger
    together!"

"We are the granddaughters of the witches you
    couldn't burn"

"Real men are allies, not all lies"

"I grab back"

"I've seen sturdier cabinets at Ikea!"

"So Bad, even introverts are here"

"Tweet Women with Respect"

"We Shall Overcomb!"

"Literally everything about this is so awful that I have no idea where to even start"

"Keep your Laws off my Body"

"Ninety, Nasty, and Not Giving Up!"

"Same Sh*t, Different Century" [Women dressed in Nineteenth Century attire]

"I Can't Believe I Still Have to Protest this F*cking Sh*t"

"I'd call him a C*nt... but He Lacks both the Depth and Warmth"

"Respect Existence or Expect Resistance"

"Your Laws will Destroy the Dreams of Millions"

"Keep your Politics off my Pussy"

"FEMPIRE Strikes Back"

"Men of Quality Don't Fear Equality"

"I March for my Daughter, her Daughters, and Our Mother Earth"

"The Future is Female; Woman Up"

"Pussy Trumps Tyranny"

"Feminism is the Radical Notion that Women are People"

"Real Men Don't Grab"

"Sexual Assault is Not a Joke→ Your Words
    Matter"

"I Do Not Like You Down my Shirt/I Do Not Like
    You Up my Skirt/I Do Not Like You Near
    my Rump/I Do Not Like You, Mr. Trump!"

By some strange freak of circumstances

and American voter frustration,

Donald J. Trump is the president of the United States,

but for the majority of us, he is not our president.

He is so much more than not our president.

He is a horrible human being and a swindler.

He is a travesty inflicted on the nation and the world.

Five million women and their supporters

protested at Women's Marches, January 21, 2017,

at home and abroad.

That's not a media fabrication or exaggeration.

That's not the pollsters getting it wrong again.

Those are cold hard facts with film footage

and pictures of posters galore.

Get it through your fat, orange head, Mr. Trump,

it's more than that we didn't vote for you,

LIBERTY BELL

we abhor you and all that you stand for,
and we will fight and protest more;
we will "not go gentle into that good night."

Dear Children

Dear Children,

Please read the Declaration of Independence and the U.S. Constitution including the Amendments and fight for an America that truly reflects those values, and try to ignore all the madness around us that seeks to destroy all that we adore about the red, white, and blue.

Dear Janey and Johnny,

Remember one must never tell lies or misrepresent the truth.

Okay, ignore the current president, and think of George Washington who couldn't lie about chopping down a cherry tree.

Dear Tamika and Dwayne,

Remember it's wrong to be racially, ethnically, or religiously bigoted.

Okay, ignore the current president, and think of Lyndon Johnson who passed key Civil Rights legislation and promoted the Great Society to end urban poverty.

81

Three Cheers for George Washington.

Dear Maria and Juan,

Remember that the Statue of Liberty welcomes the world's outcasts, "Give me your tired, your poor, Your huddled masses yearning to breathe free..."

Okay, ignore the current president, and think of Benjamin Harrison who opposed the Chinese Exclusion Act and championed a Pan American Union, seeking closer relationships with the countries of the Americas, not walls.

Dear Shahlylia and Mohammad,

Remember that the First Amendment guarantees freedom of religion.

Okay, ignore the current president, and think of Thomas Jefferson who valued freedom of religion so much he wrote it into the Bill of Rights, the first amendments to the U.S. Constitution.

Dear Susie and LaTonya,

Remember that *Roe v. Wade* protects your reproductive rights—your body, your choice.

Okay, ignore the current president, and think of Jimmy Carter, a devoted Southern Baptist and author of *A Call to Action: Women, Religion, Violence, and Power*, and

his acceptance of the need for girls and women in the U.S. and across the globe to have access to both birth control and abortion as essential to their independence and their futures.

Dear Nancy and Lavender,

Remember that the Supreme Court said that same sex marriage was as legitimate as heterosexual marriage.

Okay, ignore the current president, and think of Barack Obama and his transgendered bathroom directive and the media and public support for LGBTQIAA+ people.

Dear Children,

America is in a dark place, led by a truly frightening man, but millions of us are fighting, and we will continue to fight for ourselves and for you. America and Americans are better than this. They don't need to lie, or bully, or scape goat. They don't need to ignore scientific fact and fail to show basic civility and compassion. Oh, Children, despite our current president, you should strive to be caring and honest human beings. We must make sure that all of us can lead meaningful lives as the nature of work transforms into something out of *1984* or *A Brave New World*. Take heart, Children, this crazy situation is our wake-up call.

Dear Children,

The Republicans have succeeded in confirming Betsy DeVos as Secretary of Education, proving that they are spine-less, soul-less bastards, willing to sacrifice America's children on the altar of greed and privateering and willing to follow the Twitter Troll as he makes America a living hell.

I wish I could tell you to ignore this one, but I can't.

I wish these powerful people cared more about you, but apparently they don't.

So I will put these words on paper and hope that they count for something, even if it is only a very little, small something.

Oh, My Dear Children, may God bless you, every one of you. A weak condolence for the circumstances of the moment, but for now, I am afraid, it's the best I can do.

Truth?

What does truth even mean in the Trump Era?

"Alternative Facts"

"FAKE NEWS"

Trump speaks without regard for facts or truth;

He throws out the stereotypes that his base supporters

believe,

so Atlanta and Philadelphia

are "crime infested" and more "violent" than ever

because they are cities associated

with large populations of poor and minority people.

Ignore all the positive things about Atlanta and Philly,

poor Black people live there,

so they must be "in horrible shape and falling apart."

John Lewis, a Civil Rights leader and activist,

becomes a man of "all talk," "no action," "very sad,"

when, in fact, Lewis is a man of proven action,

with more than forty arrests in the cause

of championing Civil Rights.

But people of color,

"Truth May Be Kept Down, but Not Crushed"

whether African American, Latin American, or of Middle
Eastern origin,
in Trump speak, are not the face of the nation;
they are suspect, at best, and alien and undesirable to his
base.
They are people to contain, to build walls against, to keep
out, or to let suffer in the hell-holes "they've created" or rot
in jail.
Because poverty is a failure of character, according to
Trump, not a systematic problem of changing demographics
and a changing global economy.

Americans desperately want to believe that our nation is a
great country, but George W. Bush turned us into a rogue
nation with a pre-emptive war in Iraqi based on lies.
Trump simply takes it further with his lies spouted as truth,
"Alternative Facts," and if we tweet it in all caps,
"FAKE NEWS," then it must be true.

We are a nation clinging to "ranting," "lying" bully,
whose wife ironically has said she will combat cyber-
bullying.

Does that mean she can save us from her husband,
the Twitter Troll and one of the biggest cyber-bullies of all?
America is and can be great,
but not through fear, hate, and stereotypes,
only through real truth, difficult discussions about our
future, and collective action to build a future for all of us,
not just for the Trump base and not just for the United
States.

It's time to call "alternative facts"
and "FAKE NEWS" what they are,
lies, even if presented in call caps.

Earth Day Marches (Saturday April 22, 2017)

Across the nation and across the globe

people turned out in droves and droves

to champion Science and Mother Earth

because Climate Change is real and

Science should drive policy

not be under attack through White House policy.

There's a small smattering of what the protesters said:

> Society should worry when Geeks have to Demonstrate!

> Nerds of the World Unite!

> What Do We Want? Science Based Policy/When Do We Want It? After Peer Review

> In Peer Review We Trust

> Think While It is Still Legal

> Mr. Tweet-in-Chief; Science Made Tweeting Possible

> Does this Ass [picture of Trump] Make My Country Look Small

SAVE THE
EARTH

LITERALLY
EVERYTHING
DEPENDS UPON IT.

Act Now or Swim Later [bottom portion with blue waves]

Less Invasions; More Equations

Alternative Facts Are [square root symbol over -1]

Trust In Scientific Facts, Not Alternative Facts

[Pi symbol] Is All the Irrationality I Need

Ice Has No Agenda; It Just Melts

What Happens in the Arctic, Doesn't Stay in the Artic

Yo Momma's so Hot, She Is about to experience Desertific Action and Rising Sea Levels

The Oceans Are Rising and So Are We

Explain to Future Generations, It Was Good for the Economy, When They Can't Farm, Breathe the Air, and Drink the Water

Science is the Cure for Bullsh*t

Didn't die of Small Pox, Polio, or Measles? Thank Science

Science Saves Lives

I [heart] Science

Science Is for Everyone

Science Doesn't Lie!

Science, Not Silence

93

Yes to Science, No to Alternative Facts

Facts not Fox

Alternative Facts Are for Quacks

I Can't Believe I'm Marching for Facts

Make America Hypothesize Again

May the Facts Be With You

When Voldemort is President, We Need a Nation of
Hermiones

"Unless Someone Like You, Cares a Whole Awful
Lot, Nothing Is Going to Get Better; It's
Not"—Dr. Seuss

America Runs On Science

Only in America Do We Accept Weather Predictions
from a Rodent but Deny Climate Change
Evidence from Scientists

Ignorance is Curable

There Are No Jobs on a Dead Planet [image of
earth]

Respect Existence Or Expect Resistance

What I Stand For Is What I Stand On

No Drills/No Pipelines/[heart] our [image of earth]

It's the Environment, Stupid

This mother [downward pointing arrow] Is with This
　　　Mother [arrow pointing at an image of earth]

I'm with Her [arrow pointing at an image of earth]

Mother Nature Trumps Alternative Facts

One Planet, One Future

I do not like this Donald Twit/I do not like him just
　　　one bit/I do not like his funky hair/I do not
　　　like that he don't care/I do not like that he
　　　thinks strange science facts on climate
　　　change/I do not like his 50s views about a
　　　woman's right to choose/I do not like the
　　　way he speaks and insults everyone he
　　　meets/I do not like his lies and tricks/I do
　　　not like his head of bricks/I do not think he is
　　　smart/I think he's only just a fart

It was a rainy, soggy day on America's east coast,

but that didn't stop a huge turn-out in places like

Washington, DC, Philadelphia, New York, Boston,

over 10,000 people protesting across the nation and across

the Globe from Chicago, Portland, and San Francisco to

London, Tokyo, Cape Town, Berlin, and New Zealand to

Neumayer-Station in Antarctica,

over 600 marches in addition to Washington, DC,

96

where even Bill Nye, the Science Guy,

was on hand to defend science and the planet.

Too bad Mr. Trump doesn't care about the future of the

planet and doesn't appreciate the power of scientific funding

for the STEM (science, technology engineering, and

mathematical) achievements we have today.

He cares about impossible and impractical walls

and a military build-up that is reintroducing the globe to

Brinksmanship when that is not what we need at all.

Vengeance Is a Cancer

When will we learn that Vengeance is a cancer,

corrosive and caustic,

resulting in festering hatred and anger,

failing to deliver the healing balms

of forgiveness and release.

Radical love is what we need, across race, class,

gender orientation, ethnicity, and nationality.

There is no Mars Option; there is only this small,

frail planet which we are failing.

The choices we make here and now will determine our

future. Will it be "Hot, Flat, and Crowded"?

Land of misery for the bulk of humanity

with the very rich walled off in secure compounds

and underground bunkers?

Or will it be land we've struggled to create:

an open-global-society that finally accepts and understands

that, with only one planet, there is only one future.

A land that sees the need for a redistribution of wealth,

social justice for everyone, and our obligation to do the most

for this planet and her flora and fauna as best we can.

Vengeance is a cancer,

twisting and sickening our moral and physical DNA,

festering and poisoning the American way.

Championed by the Orange Menace,

a man known as a practitioner of vengeance and vendetta,

a horrifying manifestation of American failure to

meaningfully confront the complicated problems that

the nation and the globe now face.

With Trump, America has planted her proverbial head

in the sand—hoping against hope for a nostalgic return

to some idealized glory days that never actually were.

Is it so hard to move past vengeance and embrace

an uncertain future as brothers and sisters?

They call themselves responsible stewards of this precious

planet;

Why is it so hard to embrace a radical love instead of

cancerous sound bites of "America First"

and "Make America Great Again"?

I just hope we are not too late.

Oh Heartland

I saw an advertisement today,

to tour the Mississippi and the Heartland,

and all I could do was stare at it.

The Heartland handed the presidency

to a charlatan—a psychopathic liar—

a misogynistic, homophobic, xenophobic, narcissist.

Oh Heartland, automation killed manufacturing jobs

and won't bring them back, at least to humans,

despite Trump's claims.

Oh Heartland, coal and dirty energy will kill

your children and theirs. Climate change is real,

and we aren't doing enough to try and stop it.

Oh Heartland, White Power is an illusion

and will be gone by 2045

when Whites will be in the minority.

Oh Heartland, the Republicans court you
by feeding into your insecurities and fears,
"tough on crime" because
those minorities are "bad hombres,"
small government because big government
tells us what to do.

Oh Heartland, the Republican agenda is
intolerant of women's reproductive rights and
non-heterosexual unions because
liberated women and LGBTQ+ people
are threatening the stability of the family
and our children's values, but that simply isn't true.
Remember, equality and justice for all, not just the few.

Oh Heartland, our problems are bigger
and more complex than sound bites.
We need broad, sweeping, social programs
because the world is changing in ways no one
can fully imagine— a workerless world;
we need programs so that no one is left behind

and all of us can have meaningful lives even as
traditional work, as we know it, disappears.

Oh Heartland, FDR called for the Four Freedoms,
not just for Americans but for people of all nations.
Freedom of speech and religion and
freedom from want and fear.
Martin Luther King, Jr.,
highlighted "freedom from want" in his
"A Freedom Budget for All Americans" in 1967.
Why don't we have freedom from want
and freedom from fear today?
Because we pit ourselves against each other
and don't seek compromise, generosity, charity, empathy, or
reconciliation.

Oh Heartland, the future isn't empty Trump promises
using language full of fear and hate.
Trump's future is not and will not be livable and
sustainable, unless it is founded on love, compassion,

empathy, generosity, and kindness.

Let's face it together, the red and the blue.

Let's end this divide so the country can grow

or the strife that's growing will rip us apart,

with the rich fleeing to their "apocalypse insurance"

residencies, whether fortified underground bunkers in the

U.S. or properties in New Zealand, and the rest of us

screwed.

Oh Heartland, it isn't blue state folks you have to fear,

it's corporate greed, the lack of a social net,

and politicians set on conservative, ideological principles

despite the realities confronting our people and our nation.

Oh Heartland, what will we chose to do?

It can't be us against you.

A Man Who Needs To Be Impeached: President Trump

National Disaster: President Trump

Global Menace: President Trump

Nuclear War Threat: President Trump

Planet Extinction Level Event: President Trump

International Embarrassment: President Trump

Misogynist, Racist, and Narcissist: President Trump

Xenophobe and Homophobe: President Trump

Psychopathic Liar: President Trump

Classic Dunning Kruger Effect Example: President Trump

Twitter Troll: President Trump

National Disgrace: President Trump

Constant Conflict and Chaos: President Trump

A man so wrapped up in himself that he doesn't deserve to
be in the Oval Office.

A man who openly admires war criminals, dictators, and
strong men who openly kill civilians, trample Civil
Liberties, Duterte and Putin, because he wants to be
one himself.

45
MOCKERY
WORLDWIDE

For the damage he's done, No Pardon for this Clown.

So What Are We Waiting For?

Get him out of here!

He wanted to get tough on Crime, make sure he does

Jail Time!

Dump Chump Trump!

A Man Who Needs To Be Impeached: President Trump

Republican Scum

Oh, Party of Lincoln, what have these officials become?

A party of scummy elected officials, from the president

to congressmen and congresswomen to our senators.

They've traded the public good for oligarchical rule,

by the Koch brothers, the Mercers, and the like

—a white, rich, largely male, elite who don't remotely

represent the man and woman on the street and only care

about lining their own pockets.

The rich get richer, the poor get poorer,

and what's left of the middle class is screwed.

"The sound and the fury," constant conflict and chaos,

fear and hate, and the destruction of American democratic

institutions, but Republican scum don't care because they're

 in power.

"Power tends to corrupt

and absolute power corrupts absolutely."

The Trump Presidency, proves Lord Acton's words. The Republican sellouts have sold their souls to an Orange Devil. With mounting evidence of a hostile foreign power's massive tampering in the November election, something that should be seen as an act of war, Republican "tools" won't bail on a possible traitor because they won't compromise their access to power or are too cowardly to stand up to a revenge-seeking narcissist.

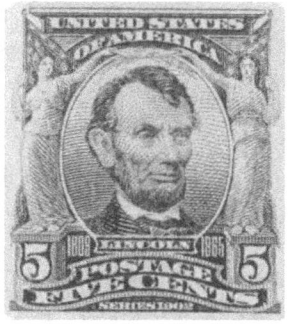

They're willing to compromise the integrity of the nation, the security of the world, the welfare of our people by following a lying, cheating, self-aggrandizing, bigoted, horrible man, rather than standing up for what is good, and true, and right.

Shame on the Republican scum!

What We've Lost

I heard Joe Biden interviewed on the radio today,
and again, I cried, for what we've lost:
civility, empathy, decency, respectability.

Trump has decimated a legacy of US policy
established since at least WWII, at home and abroad,
stewarded by leaders of both Republican and Democratic
parties.
What we've lost is humane responsibility and world
leadership.

What we've lost is democracy for oligarchical rule,
by the Koch brothers, the Mercers, and the like.
For 4.6 billion dollars, the rich bought an election.
Not a government, "by the people and for the people,"
but a government bought by Big Money interests to
enrich the corporate sector and screw the average man,
woman, and child.

And Republicans in the House and Senate

have lost their integrity and honorability
by willing abandoning those qualities
for a wild, roller-coaster ride
on the coat-tails of melomaniac
who doesn't care about democracy
or law and order, due process, or justice.
By aligning with Trump, they are abandoning
the principals that founded the nation
and aligning with racist organizations and Big Money.
They don't give a sh*t about regular Americans
as seen in their willingness to poison the environment,
gut the public schools, leave millions of Americans
without health insurance, advocate for policies that
discriminate against immigrants, minorities, women,
and the LGBT+ community.
How they can sleep at night or look the members of
their families in the face, I just don't know.

Trump doesn't really care about America.
He just cares about himself
—the unpresidential man-child,
who screams tirades at the continuously playing TVs
that line his White House,

yells obscenities at his Republican fellows,

follows all that with Twitter storms of lies, insults, and hate.

What we've lost,

the dignity of the office of the President of the United

States.

What we've lost, is the right to be a nation that is a world

leader.

The Trump administration's failure to fill thousands of

federal government jobs

threatens to paralyze the government, at home and abroad,

which could bring the whole system down.

Then, what we've lost is the whole "noble experiment,"

the longest sustained democratic government in

human history, lost under the banner of Trump.

Trump's set the nation on a childish vendetta

to undo the legacy of the first African American President.

It cripples his sense of White male privilege

to leave anything in tact whether

Obamacare, protection of the environment,

or transgender student bathroom rights.

That a significant amount of our nation's citizens

are "on board" with this destructive and reckless course

just shows how ignorant we've become and how much we've lost.

Post-Election

Essays

A Vindication of John Lewis

John Lewis, U.S. Representative of Georgia's 5th District since 1987, Civil Rights icon, the youngest of the Big Six, Chairman of the Student Nonviolent Coordinating Committee (SNCC, pronounced "snick") along with A. Philip Randolph, Founder of the Brotherhood of the Sleeping Car Porters (BSCP), James Farmer, Jr., National Director of the Congress for Racial Equality (CORE), Roy Walkins, Executive Secretary for the National Association for the Advancement of Colored People (NAACP), and Martin Luther King, Jr., President of the Southern Christian Leadership Conference (SCLC).

In 1961, John Lewis participated in the Freedom Rides, at risk to his personal safety and security. In 1965, marching in Selma, Alabama, he was struck in the head by a state trooper's nightstick. He had his head split open, suffered a concussion, and was rendered unconscious. He woke up in a hospital. John Lewis continued his work in SNCC, in the Civil Rights Movement and beyond, becoming known as the "conscience of the U.S. Congress." He has been arrested more than forty times while championing civil rights causes. He has been physically attacked and seriously injured performing nonviolent acts of protests. John Lewis is an activist, a man of action and words, and an American hero.

On November 9th, 2016, more than half the U.S. population was not just disappointed by Trump's election but truly horrified at the prospect. We wept. Some of us protested. Some of us are still protesting. Some of us write out our protests in poems, essays, and/or stories. We are organizing and figuring out what to do to take back elections in 2018 and 2020. John Lewis was protesting when he said on *Meet the Press* that he could not see Donald Trump as a legitimate president because of the Russian meddling with the election both on behalf of Trump and against Hillary Clinton, valid concerns according to the FBI and the Department of Homeland Security. Lewis was exercising his First Amendment right to freedom of speech. He also said that he would not be attending the inauguration, the first he will miss in thirty years. These may be unusual moves by a sitting member of the House of Representatives, but they are legitimate forms of protest in keeping with Lewis' legacy of nonviolent protest.

However, in the Trump Era, any criticism against Trump results in vitriol from the Twitter Troll Supreme. So the attacks on Lewis spewed forth: "all talk," "no action," and "very sad." As always, Trump tweets without researching the actual truth or thinking about the consequences of his words. "All talk" and "no action" are just ridiculous and blatantly inaccurate ways to describe Lewis—a man of decisive action—a man willing to repeatedly put himself in harm's way to fight for what is right—a man who has been physically beaten for taking such actions. So what are Trump's tweets—"FAKE NEWS," blatant inaccuracies, insulting remarks and attacks on anyone who disagrees with him—everything un-presidential. They are tactics to distract from real issues like the Russians meddling in the U.S. election, like the many still pending court cases involving Trump and his companies that will continue to march through the courts during his presidency, and like the many new court cases to be filed against him for breaking the U.S. Constitution.

SNCC, BSCP, NALC, CORE, NAACP, SCLC—do most people today recognize those acronyms beyond the NAACP? I do. Is that because I was born in 1965? Donald Trump is nearly twenty years older than I am. He should recognize the organizations and the names associated with them. But as a White boy of privilege did he care or even pay attention to the Civil Rights Movement? From his tweets, apparently not. This is a man who freely claims he has never read a book from start to finish. What kind of "educated" man is that? Educated people read about other people—fiction and nonfiction. Reading about other people makes us more human—helps us empathize with other people—helps us walk in their shoes—helps us forgive and be kind, even to those who we disagree with. Trump probably thinks getting away with reading bits and pieces of books is just "smart business practice" just as scamming out of paying your taxes for nearly twenty years through loop holes in tax laws and a good tax attorney is "smart." John Lewis is "the conscience of the U.S. Congress," in part, because he reads and writes books. He writes of his experiences and his passion for "the beloved community" in America. Trump has books, sure, but their purposes are for selling himself—not about fighting for fundamental civil rights or making the world a better place.

Trump not only inaccurately calls Lewis a man of "all talk" and "no action," but he attacks Lewis as a politician and leader of Georgia's 5th District—stating that

USA 4c
A PUBLIC THAT READS · A ROOT OF DEMOCRACY

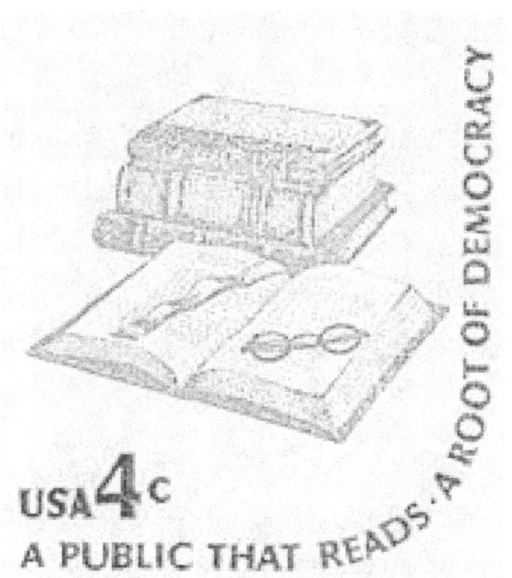

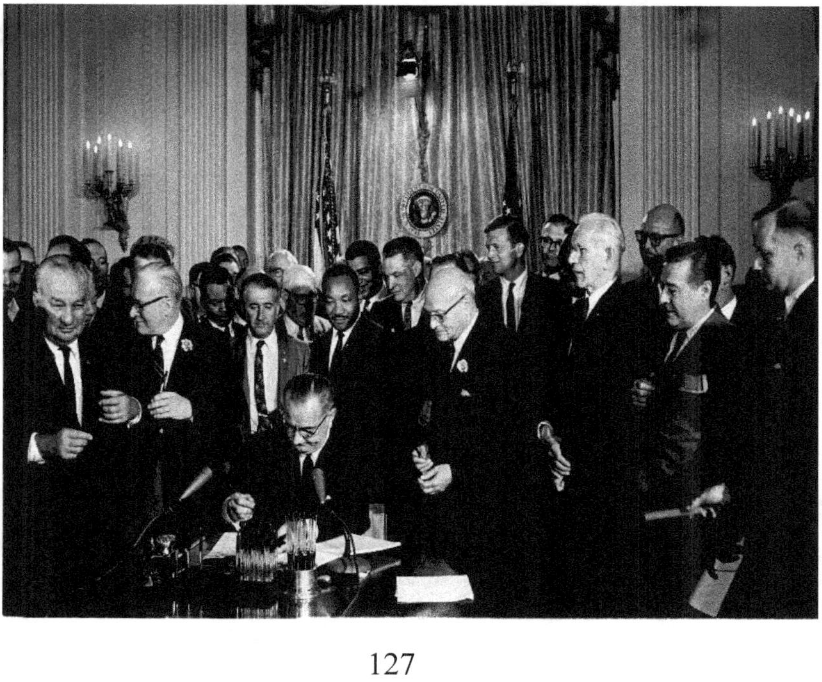

Lewis should "fix" his district which is "in horrible shape and falling apart" and "crime infested" instead of "complaining about the election results." The insulting and morally reprehensible associations that Trump makes in his tweets are the crux of our current problems. Economic inequality is what is tearing this nation apart. The rich— white, black, Hispanic, Asian, Native American—have more in common with each other than with the poor people of the same races. Class is the major divide blighting this country. Manufacturing jobs are gone in most significant ways—they will never really come back—in fact—we are on the eve of an automation revolution which will take out millions of service and white color jobs (fully automated Wendy's and H&R Blocks and Medical MRI and Sonogram facilities). Questions we desperately need to be addressing are about what can people do and be paid for if they don't need to work? What is a meaningful life when it doesn't involve working? Sure, Trump and Pence have pulled out Carrier Corp for Indiana, but the GM jobs will be around because of decisions CEOs made during the Obama administration. And what happens when further automation hits the few U.S. manufactures still operating in the U.S.? Georgia's 5th District includes Metro Atlanta. Atlanta epitomizes the split between the rich and the poor; it is one of the most segregated cities in the nation with affluent Atlanta being largely white and poor Atlanta being largely black. Trump rashly equates a black congressman with a predominately black constituency—which also rashly equates to poor and black—hence his references to the city being in "horrible shape," "falling apart," and being "crime infested." When Trump is surrounding himself with racists like Steve Bannon and Jeff Sessions, is it any wonder his tweets smack with racial stereotypes and derogatory racial remarks? No, it just leaves Americans in a grim place where Civil Rights heroes like John Lewis are attacked and Trump gets more "buzz" time diverting everyone from the serious issues we need to be facing together.

AFTER A STRUGGLE, INVOLVING A QUESTION OF COLOR, SHE PUTS ON A NEW COSTUME

X

SHE BREASTED
STORM AND
TROUBLE SORE
WHEN BROTHERS ARM
'GAINST BROTHERS
BORE;
HER HOUSE AGAINST
ITSELF DIVIDED,
FOR NORTH OR SOUTH
TILL FATE DE-
CIDED;
AND LINCOLN THEN
THE UNION
SAVES;
FROM SOUTH TO
NORTH ARE
FREED THE
SLAVES.
★

UNITED STATES

130

The Media: Enemy of the People?

President Donald J. Trump has called the media,
particularly the *New York Times* and *CNN*, "the enemy of
the people." Trump, the Twitter Troll supreme, the creator
of FAKE NEWS, alternative facts, and outright lies, uses his
trumped up stories as masterful distraction from all the harm
he is doing to the country: indirectly encouraging racist
attacks; having election staff members colluding with the
Russians; refusing to reveal his tax returns; violating the
constitution; failing to liquidate his assets into a blind trust;
forcing U.S. security forces (via US tax payers) to protect
Trump Tower and other Trump properties; sabotaging
public education, protection of our environment, the ACA,
women's reproductive rights, LGBT rights, and reform of
our broken criminal justice system; and fundamentally
undermining American citizens' trust in the media, and
more.

Why does the First Amendment protect a free press?
It states explicitly:

> "Congress shall make no law respecting an
> establishment of religion, or prohibiting the free
> exercise thereof; or abridging the freedom of speech,
> or of the press; or the right of the people peaceably

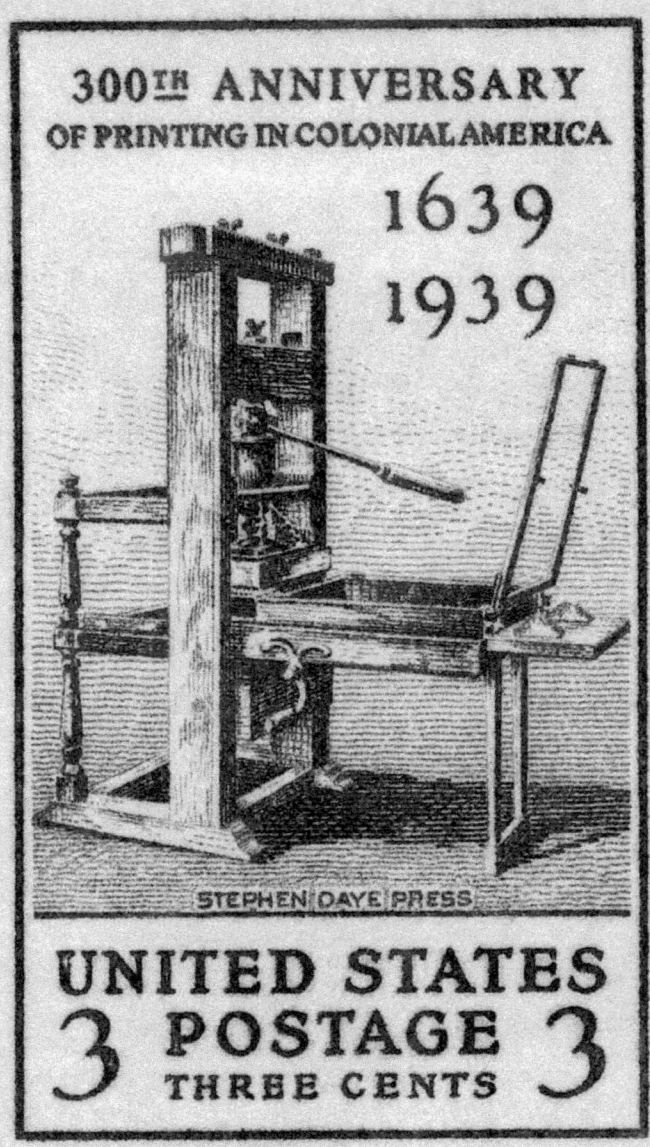

to assemble, and to petition the Government for a
redress of grievances."

What was so important to the Founding Fathers about the
freedom of the press that they forbid the government from
abridging the free press?

The free press was the instrument that could and
would inform the people of the truth and issues of the day so
that they could make informed decisions when they voted
and demanded things of their elected leaders. Without a free
press, propaganda could manipulate the population into
believing whatever a leader or a government wanted
his/her/its people wanted him/her/it to think (think of Hitler
of the 1930s and 1940s or Putin of today).

Today, the free press has been crippled by several
developments. 1) Ronald Reagan's deregulations of the
media, allowing massive media monopolies instead of
independent companies in single media mediums (radio,
TV, cable, etc.); 2) The rise of cable news, Internet news,
social media; and 3) The decline in traditional news media
(TV and newspapers).

Trump has worked aggressively to fundamentally
undermine Americans' trust in the free press at the risk of

our national security. If he can take it much further, the press, or the Gray Lady (a nickname for the *New York Times*), will become unreliable and only his rants and lies will be seen as true.

Perhaps it is worth remembering what true American patriots have said about the importance of the First Amendment and the free press.

Thomas Jefferson

"The only security of all is in a free press."

"Were it left to me to decide whether we should have a government without newspapers, or newspapers without a government, I should not hesitate a moment to prefer the latter."

"No experiment can be more interesting than that we are now trying, and which we trust will end in the establishing the fact, that man may be governed by reason and truth. Our first object should therefore be, to leave open to him all the avenues to truth. The most effectual hitherto found, is the freedom of the press. It is, therefore, the first shut up by those who fear the investigation of their actions."

Benjamin Franklin

"Whoever would overthrow the liberty of a nation must begin by subduing the freeness of speech."

George Mason

> "The freedom of the press is one of the great bulwarks of liberty, and can never be restrained but by despotic governments."

John Quincy Adams

> "The freedom of the press should be inviolate."

Herbert Hoover

> "Absolute freedom of the press to discuss public questions is a foundation stone of American liberty."

Franklin Delano Roosevelt

> "Freedom of conscience, of education, of speech, of assembly are among the very fundamentals of democracy and all of them would be nullified should freedom of the press ever be successfully challenged."

Walter Cronkite

> "Freedom of the press is not just important to democracy, it is democracy."

The freedom of the press and Americans' trust in the free press are essential for democracy and national (and global) security. President Trump seems set on threatening both of these. Additionally, with the appointment of Betsy DeVos as Secretary of Education, he seems intent on destroying public education in America.

Certainly newspapers and the free press were important instruments for wide-spread American literacy in the 17th, 18th, and 19th centuries. But formal public education for children became an additional instrument in guaranteeing an educated electorate. President John Adams, famously said in 1785, "The whole people must take upon themselves the education of the whole people and be willing to bear the expenses of it. There should not be a district of one mile square, without a school in it, not founded by a charitable individual, but maintained at the public expense of the people themselves." Universal schooling for children spread state by state and from elementary school to high schools, until by 1918, every state in the union had compulsory school attendance for at least elementary school. In recent times, the value of public education has shifted and come under attack. "A Nation at Risk" (1983) framed the value of public education in

139

America as American students being competitive with foreign students. Since then, education has been seen more and more in terms of its economic value to students and society. "The difference between a high school educated worker and a college educated worker is a million dollars"—is the classic example. This is a failure of vision. Yes, we want education to prepare our young people for the work force, but we don't want drones or automatons or robots; we want educated humans making informed decisions about their futures and the future of the country.

The true point of education in a democracy is to expose children and citizens to the free press and all of literature, philosophy, science, mathematics, and every other discipline, so that they can learn from others. They can, thus, learn from the mistakes of others. For example, who couldn't see from the American experience in Vietnam, the complicated and prolonged outcome of our most recent engagements in Iraq and Afghanistan? They can also be inspired by the works and lessons of leaders of the Progressive Movement, Franklin Delano Roosevelt, and leaders of the Civil Rights movement. FDR's Four Freedoms (Freedom of Speech, Freedom of Religion,

MAKE AMERICA THINK AGAIN!

Science is Real!

IDIOCRACY was just supposed to be a MOVIE, not a DOCUMENTARY

Freedom from Want, and Freedom from Fear (1941)) are echoed in A. Philip Randolph and Martin Luther King, Jr.'s "A Freedom Budget for All Americans" (1967).

Education, true education, is a cornerstone of the democratic way of life, and that education extends well beyond education for trade or profession. Please note, in the following quotes, how much beyond employment and economic reasons, these notables see the value of education.

Noah Webster

> "It is an object of vast magnitude that systems of education should be adopted and pursued which may not only diffuse a knowledge of the sciences but may implant in the minds of the American youth the principles of virtue and of liberty and inspire them with just and liberal ideas of government and with an inviolable attachment to their own country."

Jean Piaget

> "The principle goal of education in the schools should be creating men and women who are capable of doing new things, not simply repeating what other generations have done; men and women who are creative, inventive and discoverers, who can be critical and verify, and not accept, everything they are offered."

Edith Hamilton

> "It has always seemed strange to me that in our endless discussions about education so little stress is laid on the pleasure of becoming an educated person, the enormous interest it adds to life. To be able to be caught up into the world of thought—that is to be educated."

Iris Murdoch

> "Education doesn't make you happy. Nor does freedom. We don't become happy just because we are free—if we are. Or because we've been educated—if we have. But because education may be the means by which we realize we are happy. It opens our eyes, our ears, tells us where delights are lurking, convinces us that there is only one freedom of any importance whatsoever, that of the mind, and gives us the assurance—the confidence—to walk the path our mind, our educated mind, offers."

Malcolm X

> "Education is our passport to the future, for tomorrow belongs to the people who prepare for it today."

144

Wendell Berry

> "The complexity of our present trouble suggests as never before that we need to change our present concept of education. Education is not properly an industry, and its proper use is not to serve industries, either by job-training or by industry-subsidizing research. Its proper use is to enable citizens to live lives that are economically, politically, socially, and culturally responsible. This cannot be done by gathering or "accessing" what we now call "information"—which is to say facts without context and therefore without priority. A proper education enables young people to put their lives in order, which means knowing what things are more important than other things; it means putting first things first."

Jeanette Winterson

> "What it means to be human is to bring up your children in safety, educate them, keep them healthy, teach them how to care for themselves and others, allow them to develop in their own way among adults who are sane and responsible, who know the value of the world and not its economic potential. It means art, it means time, it means all the invisibles never counted by the GDP [Gross Domestic Product] and the census figures. It means knowing that life has an inside as well as an outside. And I think it means love."

DISCOVERY OF AMERICA BY CHRISTOPHER COLUMBUS IN 1492.

UNITED STATES

MY NATIVE LAND

Education is so much more than training students to be workers. As you can tell from this sample of writers, scholars, educators, Civil Rights leaders, and artists, public education in a democracy is tied to the First Amendment and the free press. In 1787, when the founders wrote the Constitution, there was no comprehensive system of public education nation-wide. Newspapers, lots and lots of newspapers, were the means of educating the public en mass; they ensured a literate and knowledgeable public. Alex de Tocqueville, in *Democracy in America*, said, "Thus it is in America that we find at the same time the greatest number of associations and of newspapers." Associations were organizations of men around a profession or trade. They were mutual aid associations—places where men talked about their lives, their trades, their futures, their rights. Newspapers and associations guaranteed an educated public of voting men before universal public education for children was instituted state by state. Today, newspapers and free press reporting are in decline due to the Internet and cable television. The minority of American citizens read the news through newspapers. More recently, the free press (whether traditional newspapers, the Internet, and/or cable television) is under attack from President

Trump, spewing his conspiracy theories while lambasting credible sources and people with lies that he doesn't bother to substantiate. He Tweets the most outrageous lies, like John Lewis not being a man of action or President Obama wire-tapping Trump Tower, and he successfully distracts the media and the public from his racial stereotyping of major cities like Atlanta and its residents and his ties to the Russians. Education should help Americans earn paychecks, but that is not all we are or should aspire to be. Americans should have a sense of values. Perhaps we should all read Thomas Paine's *Common Sense* or Marcus Aurelius' *Mediations* or William Penn's *Some Fruits of Solitude*, to ground us in what citizenship could or should be. Educated people see beyond sound bites and posturing. Perhaps that is the failure of American education today; we elected a man who spoke to us on fifth grade reading level, who paternalistically said he, and he alone, could fix our problems. He claimed he could return the U.S. economy of the post WWII manufacturing glory days (despite a looming automation revolution that no one is preparing for) and could make us safe by keeping out immigrants and building a wall on our southern border. Enough of us were apparently willing to believe in Trump's simplistic boasts for making

148

America great again, instead of confronting the complicated and complex future that faces us with the help of the media whose members, reporters, columnists, newscasters, and others, are largely our allies by keeping us informed on the issues of the day—defenders of freedom and truth—even if Mr. Trump doesn't understand what those words mean, and in spite of his efforts to demonize them in some kind of attempt to find an excuse for Martial Law and the suspension of citizens' Constitutional rights.

An Independent Judiciary Guarantees Our Liberties

Wake up, President Chump, and take some responsibility for the office that you bought.

We know you don't read or like to be well-informed on issues before you speak or Tweet, but you should really read the fine print of that Oath you took:

> "I, Donald John Trump, do so solemnly swear that I will faithfully execute the Office of President of the United States, and will to the best of my Ability preserve, protect and defend the Constitution of the United States. So help me God."

The courts and the free press are not enemies of the United States. They shouldn't be bullied or insulted, but respected and commended for the work they do.

This isn't a dictatorship, and you are not the CEO of the United States of America.

You are a public servant who should be answering to the wills of the people, the majority of whom did not vote for you and disapprove of most of what you are trying to do. As president of the United States, it is your job to work with

AN ORANGE MONARCH

WE CAN SUPPORT

other elected and appointed public servants in the Legislative and the Judiciary branches of the government. You have to work in concert with these people; you can't and shouldn't bully or try to dominate them. Government and politics do not function the way a business or a corporation does.

Oh, when will your base begin to see that you are nothing more than a lying, egotistical, swindling, crook who has no more business in the Oval Office than a kangaroo (and that is possibly an insult to that down-under beast)?

Wake up, America, before Trump, through brinksmanship, sheer disregard for the environment and science, and attacks on the foundational institutions of American democracy (like a free press and an independent judiciary), not only causes lasting harm to the nation and the world, but drags us into a war with North Korea and initiates nuclear war.

Judges aren't "so-called judges" just because you Tweet them so, nor are their rulings "ridiculous," unlike you. Most judges are appointed, not elected, for a reason; their duties are too important for them to be elected by popular vote, else it would be interesting to see if Neil Gorsuch would be a Supreme Court justice today. Judges

152

are supposed to be above petty politics—hence the
appointment process, especially for federal level judges who
are to be appointed by the office of the president and
confirmed by the senate. The Republicans' obstruction of
Merrick Garland as President Obama's appointment for the
Supreme Court seat of Justice Antonin Scalia went directly
against the separation of powers that the founding fathers
envisioned by the three separate branches of the government
(the Legislative, the Executive, and the Judiciary). In this
case, the Judiciary branch was missing a seat, the Executive

branch used its authority to nominate a candidate (Garland), and the Legislative branch refused their responsibility of vetting that candidate—unfairly blocking the separation of powers and unduly influencing the Judiciary appointment. In 1776, Thomas Paine made this very clear when he said:

> "The dignity and stability of government in all its branches, the morals of the people, and every blessing of society depend so much upon an upright and skillful administration of justice, that the judicial power ought to be distinct from both the legislative and executive, and independent upon both, that so it may be a check upon both, as both should be checks upon that."

The Judiciary needs to be separate from both the Legislative branch and the Executive branch, as likewise the Legislative branch needs to be separate from the Executive and the Judiciary, and the Legislative needs to be separate from both the Executive and the Judiciary. The Senate's obstruction of Garland was a direct violation of the tenants of the separation of powers. Further, candidate Trump boast about putting Neil Gorsuch on the Supreme Court, and the senate by taking the "nuclear option," has now trashed a time-honored protocol which will have unforeseen consequences. The specific alignment of all branches of the government under the erratic and bullying force of the president (the

Executive branch) has fundamentally tampered with the notion of separation of powers and points the country in a dangerous direction. Thomas Paine also said in 1776 that

"No country can be called free which is governed by an absolute power; and it matters not whether it be an absolute royal power or an absolute legislative power, as the consequences will be the same to the people."

By welding Republican power in all three branches of the government (the Legislative, the Executive, and the Judiciary), the threat to democracy in the United States is very real.

In other ways you have attempted to undermine the authority of the Judiciary. How can you attack judges for not being elected and insist on your right to appoint a Supreme Court justice? Oh, wait, it's you, Twitter Troll supreme, and you attack anyone who disagrees with you, like U.S. District Judge William Orrick, U.S. District Judge Gonzalo Curiel, or U.S. District Judge James Robart.

Perhaps it is wise to reflect a bit on what more of our founding fathers had to say about the separation of powers (legislative, executive, and judicial), and think about your failure to uphold the Constitution, and how your constant assaults on the truth, science, the press, and now the courts, threaten to destabilize this nation.

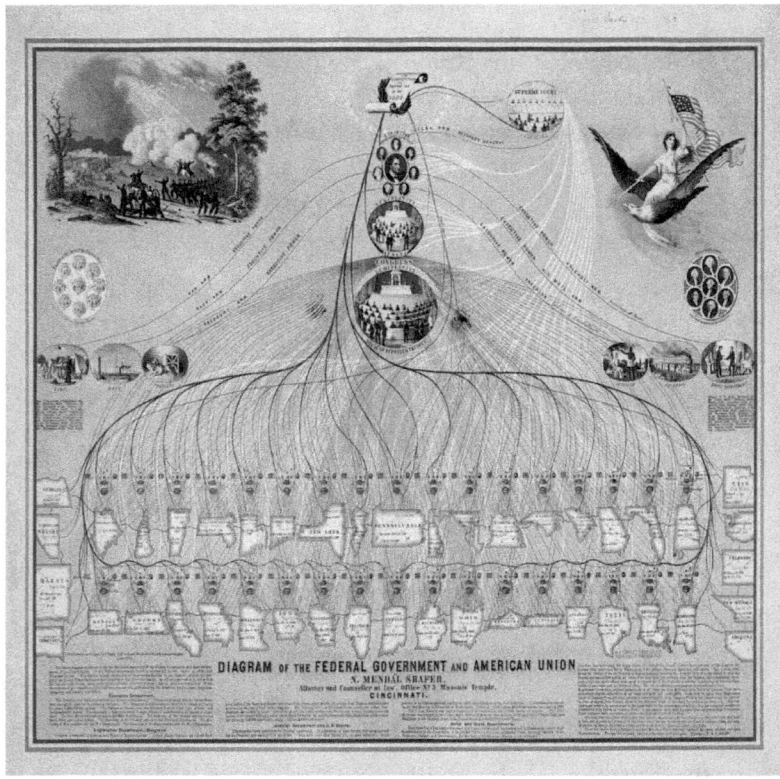

John Adams, 1776,

> "A question arises whether all the powers of government, legislative, executive, judicial, shall be left in this body? I think a people cannot be long free, nor ever happy, whose government is in one Assembly."

THOMAS PAINE
1737—1809

Thomas Paine, 1778,

> "We repose an unwise confidence in any
> government, or in any men, when we invest them
> officially with too much, or an unnecessary quantity
> of, discretionary power."

Thomas Paine, 1782,

> "I have never made it a consideration whether the
> subject was popular or unpopular, but whether it was
> right or wrong; for that which is right will become
> popular, and that which is wrong, though by mistake
> it may obtain the cry or fashion of the day, will soon
> lose the power of delusion, and sink into disesteem."

COMMON SENSE:
ADDRESSED TO THE
INHABITANTS
OF
AMERICA.
On the following interesting
SUBJECTS.

I. Of the Origin and Design of Government in general;
   with concise Remarks on the English Constitution.
II. Of Monarchy and Hereditary Succession.
III. Thoughts on the present State of American Affairs.
IV. Of the present Ability of America, with some miscellaneous
    Reflections.

Written by an ENGLISHMAN.

Man knows no Master save creating Heaven,
Or those whom choice and common good ordain.
                                        Thomson.

PHILADELPHIA, Printed.
And Sold by R. BELL, in Third-Street, 1776.

Alexander Hamilton, 1787,

"The regular distribution of power into distinct departments: the introduction of legislative balances and checks; the institution of courts composed of judges holding their offices during good behavior; the representation of the people in the legislature by deputies of their own election…. They are the means, and powerful means, by which the excellence of republican government may be retained and its imperfections lessened or avoided."

158

Richard Lee, 1787,

> "It has hitherto been supposed a fundamental maxim that in governments rightly balanced, the different branches of a legislature should be unconnected, and that the legislative and executive powers should be separate."

James Madison, 1788,

> "The accumulation of all powers, legislative, executive, and judiciary, in the same hands, whether appointed, or elective, may justly be pronounced the very definition of tyranny."

Alexander Hamilton, 1788,

> "The same rule that teaches the propriety of a
> partition between the various branches of power,
> teaches us likewise that this partition ought to be so
> contrived as to render the one independent of the
> other."

Alexander Hamilton, 1788,

> "The history of human conduct does not warrant that
> exalted opinion of human virtue which would make
> it wise in a nation to commit interests of so delicate
> and momentous a kind, as those which concern its
> intercourse with the rest of the world, to the sole
> disposal of a magistrate created and circumstanced
> as would be a President if the United States."

Alexander Hamilton, 1788,

> "The reasonableness of the agency of the national
> courts in cases in which the state tribunals cannot be
> supposed to be impartial, speaks for itself. No man
> ought certainly to be a judge in his own cause, or in
> any cause in respect to which he has the least interest
> or bias."

George Washington, 1796,

> "The necessity of reciprocal checks in the exercise
> of political power, by dividing and distributing it
> into different depositories, and constituting each the
> guardian of the public weal against invasions by the
> others, has been evinced by experiments ancient and
> modern, some of them in our country and under our
> own eyes."

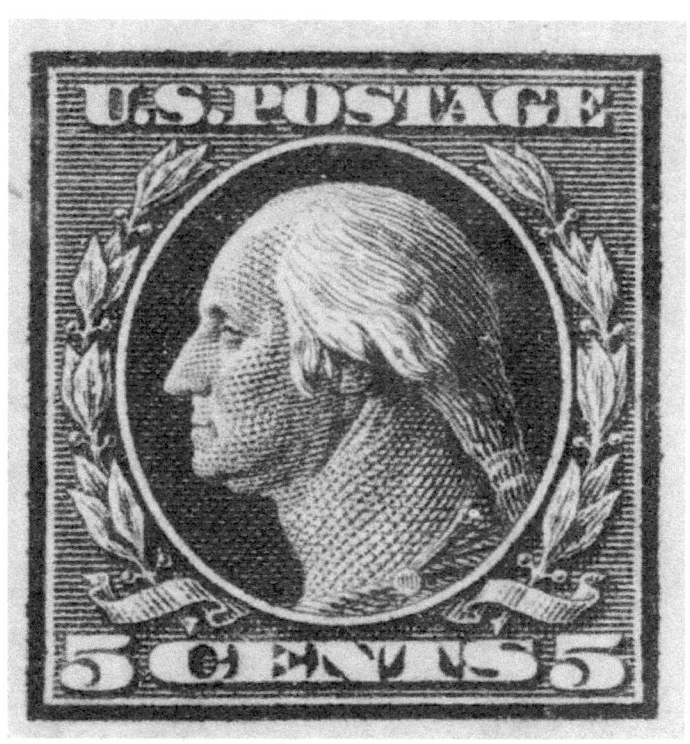

Thomas Jefferson, 1819,

> "My construction of the constitution is very different
> from that you quote. It is that each department is
> truly independent of the other, and has an equal right
> to decide for itself what is the meaning of the
> constitution in the cases submitted to its action; and
> especially, where it is to act ultimately and without
> appeal."

Thomas Jefferson, 1823,

"The principle of the Constitution is that of a
separation of legislative, Executive and Judiciary
functions, except in cases specified. If this principle
be not expressed in direct terms, it is clearly the
spirit of the Constitution, and it ought to be so
commented and acted on by every friend of free
government."

Our system, with its checks and balances, is not efficient, but that inefficiency, is our guarantee that the rights of most of our citizens are respected and that no one leader can become a strongman or strongwoman and usurp power unjustly. That must be a very frustrating thing for a control freak like you. But you are not the CEO of the country, you are not a dictator, and oath you took means that are pledged to uphold the Constitution and defend our democratic institutions even when they do things that you don't like. Back off Trump, by attacking the judiciary, you put in peril all of us.

The Journal of American History

164

Reconciling the American Pasts

> "[The Constitution] was framed upon the theory that the peoples of the several states must sink or swim together, and that in the long run prosperity and salvation are in union and not division."
> —Benjamin Nathan Cardozo

L.P. Harley opened her 1953 novel, *The Go-Between*, with the now famous statement, "The past is a foreign country; they do things differently there." It is a profoundly true statement that we perhaps underestimate. With the benefits of hindsight, we (people today) are outsiders to the past and past actors. We have knowledge, understanding, and perspective that they do not. That doesn't mean we shouldn't try to fully understand the past or that we should romanticize it or simplify it. The American past is deeply complex and filled with many actors, some of whom have been repeatedly marginalized, but who were dealing with events and issues as best they could. In a recent National Public Radio interview, Harvard historian, Jill Lepore, argued that Americans today are not just divided politically, but that they are divided over two sets of ideas about the American past. For one set, there is a need to see America as a great nation—the "city upon the hill" in the words of John Winthrop in 1630 from his "A Model of Christian Charity" sermon about the Puritan experiment in the Massachusetts Bay Colony. This is Horatio Alger's America where anyone can make it with ambition and hard work. This is America of Manifest Destiny and continuing progress. This is the America that sent troops to the War to End All Wars (WWI) and the Good War (WWII) where those troops were decisive in the positive ends of both conflicts. The people who embrace this history want to see America in this image, with a noble past; they, in fact, want to see America "great again." The messiness of the Civil Rights Movement, the Vietnam War, the Women's Movement, the Gay Rights Movement, urban poverty, and crime, among other things, disturb them because they tarnish the image of American exceptionalism and American virtue. They want an isolationist America in a globalized world. They want "America First" and Americans first.

The other set sees a more complicated and flawed American past—one with noble ideals and racism, sexism, homophobia, and xenophobia—one with both the Good War

and the Vietnam War and now the Second Iraqi War—one
with increasing poverty for the poor and with
increasing wealth for the rich—one with a radically
shrinking social net and a punitive criminal justice system
that disproportionally targets people of color and those of
lower socio-economic strata. These people are more
comfortable with a flawed American past because they are
not nostalgic for an idealized past (which included slavery
as just one example) and want to press for a better, more
inclusive future for all Americans. Danger lies in
romanticizing the American past. In not confronting the
complexities of our past, we risk making the same mistakes
instead of learning from them. For example, given what
happened in Vietnam, who couldn't see that "shock and
awe" wouldn't hand U.S. troops a "slam dunk" in the
Second Iraqi War? And who couldn't see that stigmatizing
immigrants is not only wrong but, too often, leads to vicious
attacks and racial slurs? We have stigmatized "others"
before, with ugly consequences. We need to move forward,
not back.

Remember that the American colonies were
established largely for commercial purposes. Certainly, this
was true of Virginia, established in 1607 by the Virginia

Company. But profit was the main goal, hence the adoption of the plantation model in the Southern states to maximize profits as opposed to the small family farm model favored in the Northern colonies. A minority of colonies offered religious toleration (Maryland and Pennsylvania) until the British Act of Toleration (1689) made it applicable in the colonies as well as in Great Britain.

The Northern colonies and the Southern colonies quickly developed two very different agricultural styles, which would inevitably bring them into conflict. The South developed plantation farming systems that were dependent first on indentured servant labor and then on slave labor while the North developed small independent family farms that, when necessary, employed free labor. Cities, North and South, grew to have large classes of craftsmen, merchants, inn keepers, and others. Port cities had shipping related-businesses, sailors and captains, merchants, and services to accommodate commerce and trade.

Products of their times, colonists and the founding fathers of what would become the United States of America, were racists, elitists, and sexists. They, meaning elite white men, were toying with liberal ideas from the Enlightenment, but they also believed in the Great Chain of Being (see first image in this essay), a hierarchical ranking of all creation with God at the pinnacle, and then, in descending order by rank, the Nine Choirs of Angels (Seraphim, Cherubim, Thrones, Dominions, Virtues, Powers, Archangels, Principalities, and Angels). Then, the races of men from the most "refined" and intelligent" (i.e., Northern European whites and their descendants) to the most "primitive" and "savage" (i.e., races of color). This "lower" assessment of the colored races was reinforced by their lack of advanced technology and culture (see second and third images, be mindful that the second image hung in The American Museum of National History while the third appeared in an 1870 textbook). Thus, colonists' contact with Native Americans often led to conflict, and when Native American populations were decimated by European diseases like Small Pox (which the colonists had brought with them), the colonists wrongly interpreted these diseases and their impacts has God's hand wiping out the colonists' heathen and savage enemies and confirming that North American settlement was the destiny of colonists.

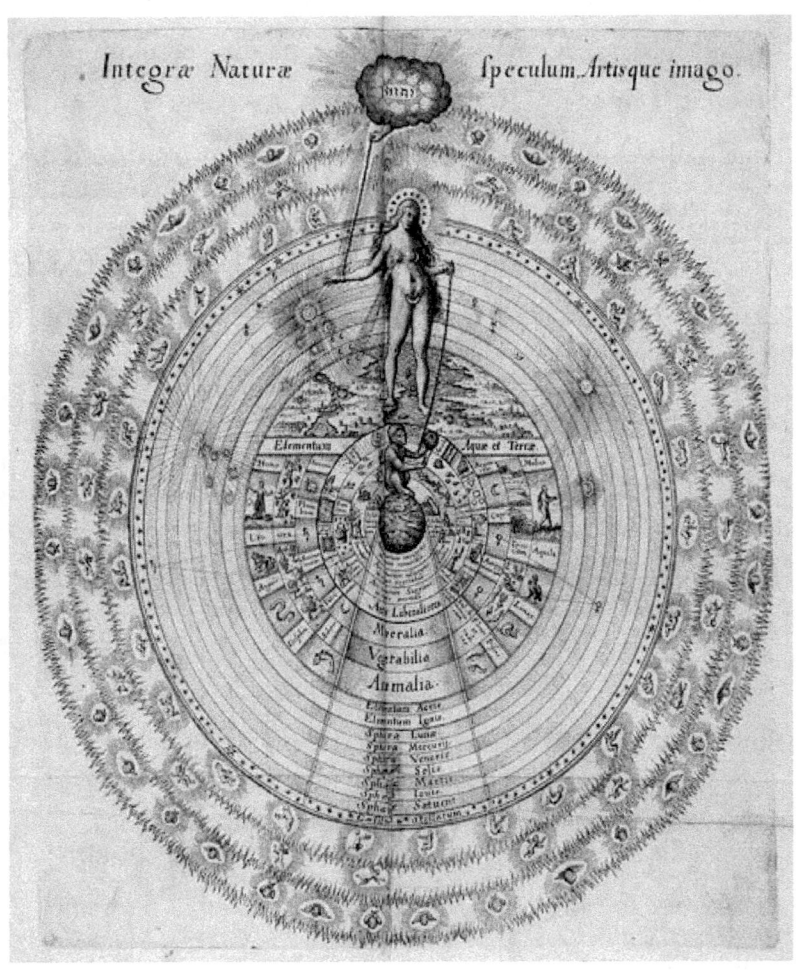

See Wayne Schumaker's paragraph description of this Great Chain of Being image at the end of the essay.

In other words, God was punishing the sinful heathens and opening up Christian settlement to the white colonists.

The slave trade was well established before the first slaves were shipped to Virginia. But as health conditions improved for colonists and their indentured servants, African slaves proved to be more economically sound investments, and the racial prejudice was already in place to make any other relationship between white masters and black slaves unthinkable.

When relations between the colonists and England became tense, the founding fathers found themselves contemplating a new form of government inspired by Enlightenment ideas—a form of government like the brief experiment with democracy in Athens of Ancient Greece and the also brief experiment with a republic in Ancient Rome. Yet when they wrote in the Declaration of Independence,

> "When in the Course of human events it becomes necessary for one people to dissolve the political bands which have connect them with another and to assume among the powers of the earth, the separate and equal station to which the Laws of Nature and of Nature's God entitle them, a decent respect to the opinions of mankind requires that they should declare the causes which impel them to separation. We hold these truths to be self-evident, that all men

171

are created equal, that these are Life, Liberty, and the pursuit of Happiness.—That to secure these rights, Governments are instituted among Men, deriving their just powers from the consent of the governed,—That to secure these rights, Governments are instituted among Men, deriving their just powers from the consent of the governed"

they didn't really mean all men, and they didn't mean women at all. After the ratification of the U.S. Constitution, only white landowning men could vote, but that changed over time as more and more people were granted suffrage.

Of course, today we know that race has nothing to do with intelligence and that discrimination is wrong. There is no Great Chain of Being, and many of us question the idea of God's existence. Slavery is wrong—on so many levels—and yet there is a flourishing illegal slave trade today—even within the U.S. What does that say about us?

The scar of racial bigotry still is not healed today as evidenced by the disproportionate number of minorities shot by police, in poverty, in prison, and unemployed. How the Native Americans were treated was wrong too, but the lens of racism allowed these things to happen. Of course, there were always some who saw the humanity in "others." Some Quakers always championed Abolition and the fair

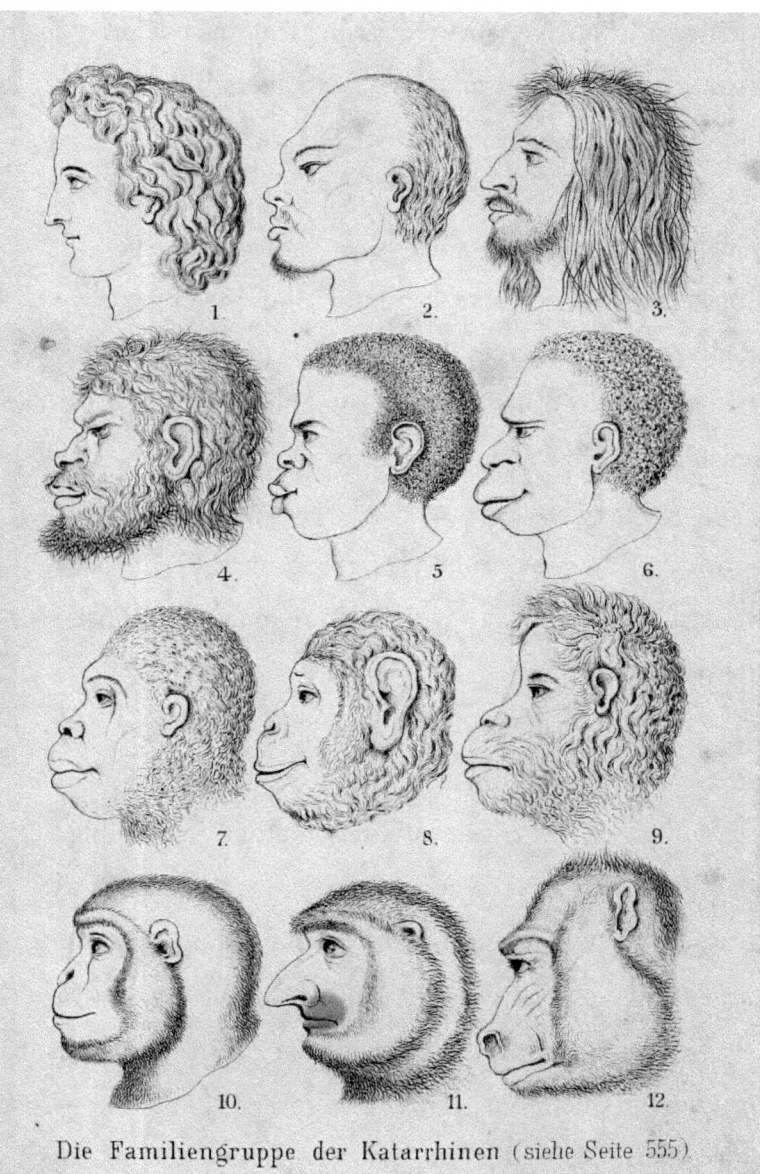

Die Familiengruppe der Katarrhinen (siehe Seite 555)

treatment of Native Americans, and that number grew over time. That doesn't mean that slave holders were devils and Northerners were saints. The vast majority of Northerners and Southerners were bigots, in a belief system that sanctioned that bigotry, but some Northerners and Southerners were worse than others. And then there were contradictions. Thomas Jefferson was the author of the the Declaration of Independence, a founding father, the third president of the United States, and the designer of Monticello. By today's standards, he would also be considered a sexist, elitist, racist, human trafficker, and rapist. (His relationship with Sally Hemings is ultimately defined by her status as his chattel.)

Much of documented history tells the story of great men (and a few women) and major events and circumstances. It is, therefore, hard but not impossible to reconstruct the lives of people who did not document themselves: most women, working class people, simple farmers, slaves, Native Americans, children, and others.

Another aspect of telling history is that the alien and the new are often threatening, different, and strange. African slave names were different and "ugly" to whites, so slaves were given Christian names or even the names of Ancient

Greeks or Romans. African languages and religions were alien and incomprehensible to whites, so Africans were converted to Christianity and forced to speak English. We seek sameness, which seems safe and comfortable, rather than difference, which can seem threatening and dangerous. However, different is just different; it doesn't need to be threatening and scary. In fact, this is largely what the First Amendment is about. Freedom of religion is about no state being able to impose a religion on any one individual. Each private citizen was free to choose his/her religion and practice it as he or she chose within the confines the tenants of his or her religion and the law.

Go back to the early colonies. The New England colonies (those off shoots of Massachusetts, Connecticut, Rhode Island, and New Hampshire) were fierce Calvinists and were rather intolerant of others attempting to preach other religions within their borders. Pennsylvania and Maryland were outliers with their tolerance for religious freedom, at least until the 1689 British Act of Tolerance made it law for Britain and all her colonies.

Advance to the 1930s and listen or read Franklin Delano Roosevelt's speeches; they are full of Biblical references. Why? Not because the federal government

The Mongolian [Chinese] Octopus

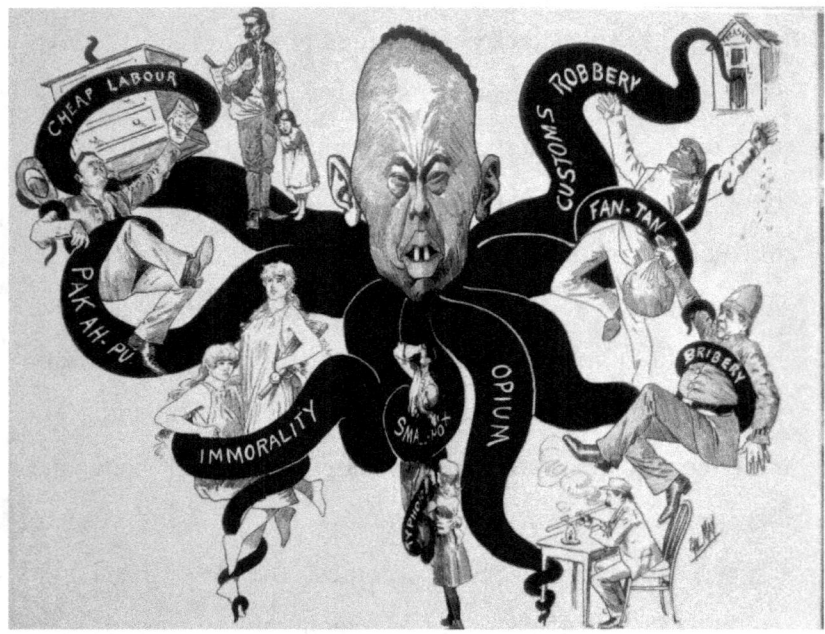

Tentacles of the Mongolian/Chinese Octopus: Cheap Labor, Pak Ah-Pu (Chinese Lottery)(Gambling), Immorality (Prostitution), Small Pox/Typhoid (Disease), Opium, Bribery, Fan-Tan (another form of Chinese gambling), Customs Robbery.

[Disclosure: "The Mongolian [Chinese] Octopus" is a 19th Century Australian political cartoon. However, if one looks at the Thomas Nast political cartoons that appeared in *Harper's Weekly* ("Let the Chinese Embrace Civilization, and They May Stay" (1882), "Pacific Chivalry" (1869), and "Ah Sin Was His Name" (1879)), one can see the same ugly racist sentiments as the Australian cartoon. I chose this substitution because "The Mongolian [Chinese] Octopus" fit so well with "The Papal Octopus" and "The Destructive Mormon Monster."]

imposed Christianity on all citizens, but because most Christian Americans knew their Bibles inside and out and "Civic Religion" was an accepted aspect of national life. Poor people, those hit hardest by the Great Depression, might not know references to classical or well-known authors, but they knew their Bible, and FDR used that to make connections to people in his speeches. The common "cultural literacy" of the 1930s and 1940s for most Americans was the Bible despite the fact that not all Americans were Christian. Today, such Biblical references would be problematic for several reasons. First, most Americans today don't know their Bible. Second, separation of Church and State—fundamental to the Constitution— means that no one religion is endorsed by the federal government. Additionally, we are today more aware of the sensitivities of others, and respecting the separation of Church and State, we respect that people of non-Christian religions (whether Jews, Muslims, Hindus, Buddhists, or others) do not appreciate Christianity imposed on them through such rhetoric and language in political speeches.

Similarly, if we look at the language of the speeches of Martin Luther King, Jr., during the 1950s and 1960s, we also see many Biblical references. This is in part due to his being a Southern Baptist minister, but it also because African Americans of the 1950s and 1960s were poorer and less well-off than their white peers, and the common "cultural literacy" that bound them together was the Bible. Today, again with awareness and sensitivity that we have now, most political and national leaders do not draw on religion in appealing to the public because of the separation of Church and State, unless they are trying to delegitimize freedom of religion as Trump and the Alt-Right are attempting to do by banning Muslims and covertly encouraging religious and racial hate crimes.

Today some Americans lament prayer disappearing from public school or nativities and religious imagery as part of the decoration of public and government buildings. This is not disrespectful. In fact, it is the mark of respect. Separation of Church and State and freedom of religion mean that private citizens have the rights to celebrate holidays, religious or otherwise, in any way they choose in private, in and on their homes, trees, etc. But public and government buildings and organizations must stay neutral on religion, and that includes religious holidays. Thus, during winter holidays, religiously neutral decorations can include snowflakes, snowmen and snowwomen, candles, poinsettias, holly leaves and berries, but they can't include religious imagery or nativities. Churches and synagogues as religious organizations are free to decorate religiously, but that's it. This is not an assault on Christian values but a re-affirmation of the First Amendment.

The choice to worship any religion one choses is guaranteed by the First Amendment. Though most Americans are Christians, we have significant populations of Jews, Muslims, Hindus, Buddhists, Atheists, and others. These are legitimate choices and are not and should not be seen as bad, un-American, or even anti-American. Research these religions. At their cores, all have very similar goals of helping believers or adherents to be the best human beings that they can be and to advance the betterment of the human race. Different is just different; it doesn't need to be threatening or scary, and in the best circumstances, up a whole new way of looking at things—full of new possibilities that we hadn't realized were there before. There are bad apples in every barrel; that doesn't mean dumping the barrel. Extremists have always done crazy and, often, very harmful things. How many billions of lives have been

"History Repeats Itself" by Watson Heston

"And he cried in a loud voice saying, 'My God, my God,
why hast thou forsaken me?'"
"This is the U.S. in the Hands of the Jews"

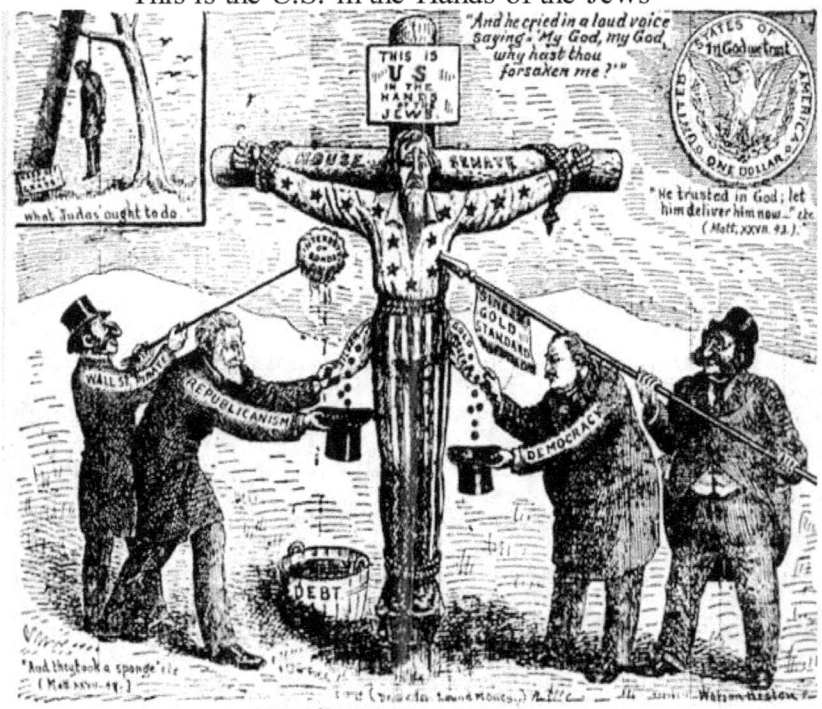

HISTORY REPEATS ITSELF.

"What Judas ought to do"

"He trusted in God; let him deliver him now"
Matthew 27: 43

"House" "Senate" (arms of the cross)

Wall Street Pirates, Republicanism, Insterest on Bonds, Silver,
Gold, Gold Standard, Democracy
"Debt"(bucket)

sacrificed in the name of one god or another? Jihadists do not represent the bulk of Muslims. In 1572 in France, Charles IX set in motion mass violence by Catholics against the French Protestants, the Huguenots, where perhaps 11,000 people were killed in the St. Bartholomew's Day massacre. Closer to our own times, Jim Jones (born in Indiana) as leader of the Peoples Temple Agricultural Project had 918 of his followers commit suicide in Jonestown, Guyana, in 1978.

Religious extremists will always exist, and people will kill in the name of religion, despite the vast majority of religious believers being peaceful and content to practice their religious beliefs, customs, rituals, and traditions within the contexts of their established religious organizations, other appropriate organizations, and their homes. But we cannot condemn whole religions or nations for the beliefs of some extremists or their leaders/leadership we disagree with. America's past contains examples of racial, religious, and ethnic bigotry that are distasteful to us today (in particular, see "History Repeats Itself," the "Chinese Octopus," the "Mormon Monster," and "The Papal Octopus").

181

"How long will this destructive monster be allowed to live?"

Victims of the Mormon Monster: Public School System, YMCA, Catholic Church, Justice, Ireland, Independent New Party, Public Opinion.

Today we should be past such bigotry, and that means no stigmatizing immigrants whether from predominantly Muslim countries or Latin America, so no travel ban and no wall. It means not tolerating and vigorously punishing hate crimes like the one committed by Jeremy Christian in Portland, that left two men dead, one injured, and two young women shaken or the one at the University of Maryland where Sean Urbanski murdered Lt. Richard Collins III. People from different races or religious are just different; they don't need to be scary or threatening. Their lives matter and should be respected and protected. Americans are bigger than fear and hate. As Cardozo reminds us, we are all in this together. A better image for us at this start of the 21st century is "Americans All, Immigrants All" (see the last image).

THE PAPAL OCTOPUS.

Romanism is a Monster, with arms of Satanic power and strength, reaching to the very ends of the earth, the arm of superstition crushing the American child, that of subversion crushing the American Flag, that of bigotry crushing the American Public School, that of ignorance crushing the credulous dupe, that of corruption crushing the law of the land, that of greed grasping public moneys, that of tyranny destroying freedom of conscience, freedom of speech, freedom of the press, all over the world—*per totam orbem terrarum.*

The Papal Octopus—Romanism is a Monster, with arms of Satanic power and strength, reaching to the very ends of the earth, the arms of superstition crushing the American child, that of subversion crushing the American Flag, that of bigotry crushing the credulous dupe, that of corruption crushing the law of the land, that of greed grasping public moneys, that of tyranny destroying freedom of conscience, freedom of speech, freedom of the press, all over the world—*per totum orbem terrarium* (one throughout the world).

That also translates to people at home who are different. Margaret Mead in 1949 in *Male and Female* wrote the following:

> "We are laying the foundations of a way of life that may become so world-wide that it will have no rivals, and [human beings'] imaginations will be both sheltered and imprisoned within the limits of the way we build. For in order to think creatively, [human beings] need the stimulus of contrast. We know by sad experience how difficult it is for those who have been reared within one civilization ever to get outside its categories, to imagine, for instance, what a language could be like that had thirteen genders. Oh, yes, one says, masculine, feminine, and neuter—and what in the world are the other ten? For those who have grown up to believe that blue and green are different colours it is hard even to think how any one would look at the two colours if they were not differentiated, or how it would be to think of colours only in terms of intensity and not of hue…. We stand at the moment in history when we still have choice, when we are just beginning to explore the properties of human relationships."

In 1949, this renowned American anthropologist could see the future of gender fluidity in a way that we are just beginning to grapple with as a nation today. People who identify as LGBTQQIAA+ are just different. Consider this, that the likelihood of a child being born transgender is the same as that of a child being born with red hair. That means that transgender people are much more common that we realize. It also means that they have been forced into the de facto categories of "male" and "female" and not allowed to explore an identity somewhere in between. Nearly seventy years ago, Mead could see this possibility; isn't it time we did too? Being different doesn't have to be scary or threatening. Allowing LGBTQQIAA+ people to express themselves doesn't mean they are trying to make everyone the ways they are; it just means that we allow them space to be who they are. Acceptance of LGBTQQIAA+ people is not an attack on our religions or families. In fact, it is just the opposite. Our narrow definitions of "male" and "female," often religiously endorsed, and our assumptions of normative heterosexuality just need to be expanded to be more inclusive. For too long, LGBTQQIAA+ identities have been criminalized or psychopathologized. Just like our knowledge and sensitivity about racial and ethnic inferiority has changed and been enlightened for the better and for a more humane world where all have equal rights, we need to expand our acceptance of LGBTQQIAA+ people too. The First Amendment begins with freedom of religion and the inappropriateness of government imposing a religion on citizens: "Congress shall make no law respecting an establishment of religion, or prohibiting the free exercise thereof." Religion and decisions about one's personal life based on religious beliefs are private affairs. It is not right for people to try to impose their religious beliefs on others. If you believe in something or don't believe in something, you have every right to act according to your beliefs (within the confines of the law), but you should not try to impose your beliefs on others who may have very different beliefs and practices. Further, government policies and legislation should not be dictated by imposing religious beliefs on the public.

As we gain knowledge and understanding, our views change. For example, as late as the 1970s, the Catholic Church saw pro-creation as being a central part of any marriage. So important was this aspect of marriage, that the Church would not condone the marriage of a young woman to a young man because the young man was paralyzed from the waist down. In the Church's view at the time, the marriage couldn't result in children and, thus, was not an appropriate union. Secular society had no such restriction,

so the young couple was able to marry, just not in the Church. The Catholic Church is beyond that prohibition today, but it is an example of how our attitudes change and evolve over time. Different is just different—not scary or threatening.

Perhaps even more close to home is how we deal with female reproductive rights. Again the First Amendment raises its head here. Government should not legislate based on the religious beliefs of some. People are free to act on their religious beliefs in terms of birth control and abortion, but they should not to impose their personal and private religious beliefs on others, and the government, federal, state, or local, should not try to legislate morality. (Remember how badly that worked with Prohibition.) *Roe v. Wade* is supported largely by the Fourth Amendment: "The right of people to be secure in their persons, houses, papers, and effects, against unreasonable searches and seizures." Women have the right to be secure in their persons; they have the right to control their fertility whether through birth control or abortion. Birth control is often a medication prescribed to a young woman or woman by a doctor; as medication, it should be paid for by health insurance, and no government policy should try to interfere with that especially if Viagra and similar erectile dysfunction drugs for men are being paid for by insurance. The hypocrisy of paying for men to be able to ejaculate while not paying for women to protect themselves from pregnancy from such ejaculations surely is more than the American people are willing to put up with and is so sexist and misogynistic that legislators should not try to do such a thing.

The Fourteenth Amendment also protects a woman's right to choose:

> "...No State shall make or enforce any law which shall abridge the privileges or immunities of citizens of the United States; nor shall any State deprive any person of life, liberty, or property, without due process of law; nor deny to any person within its jurisdiction the equal protection of the laws."

Women under the Fourteenth Amendment are guaranteed both due process under the law and authority over their lives and liberties. Don't like abortion, fine don't have one, but don't impose your morality on young women and women who you know nothing about. Are you willing to help with the enormous financial and emotional burdens of having unwanted children? No? Then women must have the right to choose, and no one should be trying to take that right away. It is not the place of government to legislate morality. A

fetus cannot survive outside the womb before about twenty-three weeks of gestation; most legal abortions in the United States are performed between the eighth and twelfth weeks, but American women are entitled to abortion up to twenty-four weeks, although the vast majority of women abort before that. Forty-three point one million Americans live in poverty according to statistics, but many argue that the federal poverty line is too high, so that it doesn't accurately capture the true scope of poverty in America. Fourteen point five million children live in poverty. Nearly half (45%) of pregnancies in the United States are unplanned. A driving factor in poverty is women's inability to control their fertility and to make choices about having children. One-third of all American women (whether Caucasian, African American, Hispanic, Asian, or Native American) live at or below 200% of the federal poverty line. Activists, from Melinda Gates to Jimmy Carter to the World Health Organization (WHO), who are working to end poverty, nationally and globally, cite female reproductive control (access to birth control and abortion) as central to ending poverty. Abortion is difficult, but it is a choice that some women desperately need to have available as a viable and legal option when abortion is legal and safe. In *Roe v. Wade*, the justices fully recognized the difficulty of making a decision on this issue, stating, "We forthwith acknowledge our awareness of the sensitive and emotional nature of the abortion controversy." But they continued, endorsing an unemotional review of the issues involved, "Our task, of course, is to resolve the issue by constitutional measurement, from of emotion and of predilection." The justices emphasize not only the necessity of taking emotion out of this decision but also taking bias out of the decision. With separation of Church and State, religious bias cannot be brought to bear on a woman's right to choose.

Further, making abortion illegal won't end the need for abortion. It will only create a market for illegal abortions or back-alley abortions. When abortion is legal, it is safe. When abortion is illegal, it is too often unsafe. Whether from self-induced abortion or back-alley abortion, women risk infection, sterility, permanent injury, puncture, hemorrhage, and death. Women have thrown themselves down staircases, poisoned themselves by ingesting chemicals like bleach, lye, gunpowder, turpentine, and other substances. They have tried to probe themselves with metal knitting needles and wire coat-hangers. They have sought out abortionists who have tried to perform the abortions with crude instruments like knitting needles and coat-hangers in often less than sanitary conditions. Some abortionists inject bleach and other toxic chemicals into uterus to induce miscarriage. To make matters worse, women who have illegal abortions often do not come forward quickly (due to the shame of undergoing an illegal procedure) when the abortion has gone wrong. So their infections and the damage that has been done to them through a botched abortion is that much worse when they are forced into emergency rooms or emergency care. We can't go back to maternal deaths due to illegal abortions. Women need the right to choose. Ultimately, a woman's life is more important than the fetus.

> "No woman can call herself free who does not own and control her own body. No woman can call herself free until she can choose consciously whether she will or will not be a mother"
> —Margaret Sanger.

> "We need to support all women's ability to terminate a pregnancy and not demand that they tell us a story of victimhood in order to gain access to abortion"
> —Tracy Weitz.

> "Women are not an interest group. They are mothers, and daughters, and sisters, and wives. They are half of this country and they are perfectly capable of making their own choices about their

health"—Barack Obama.

"Make America Great Again," the appeal is nostalgic. But the 1950s wasn't paradise. It was full of racism, sexism, and intolerance. World War II and Hitler's atrocities in the concentration camps made Americans and global citizens aware that Anti-Semitism was ugly and dangerous. Joseph McCarthy's witch hunts left people black-listed and unemployable. American paranoia about Communism pushed us into war in Korea, the Cuban Missile Crisis, and Vietnam. Emmitt Till at 14 years old was brutally beaten and lynched in 1955 in Mississippi for supposedly flirting with a white woman; he was so badly beaten that he isn't even recognizable (you can view images of the boy's body today, but (warning) it is hard viewing). In 1958, after having had three children and suffering postpartum depression after each birth, Adrienne Rich needed a signed letter from her husband attesting to the fact that she had produced three children and that he consented to her hysterectomy so that the doctors would perform the procedure. True, World War II stimulated business and industry and propelled the U.S. economy to unprecedented growth that would last until the 1970s when the specter of Vietnam and inflation slowed it. The G.I. Bill sent millions

195

of men into the nation's colleges and universities and other provisions helped these men buy houses with long-term, low-interest loans. There was a significant social net and college and housing for vets only increased that social net. In a significant way, the G.I. Bill middle-classized a whole generation of men and their families. It might be the equivalent today of making community college free for everyone and also providing subsidized housing.

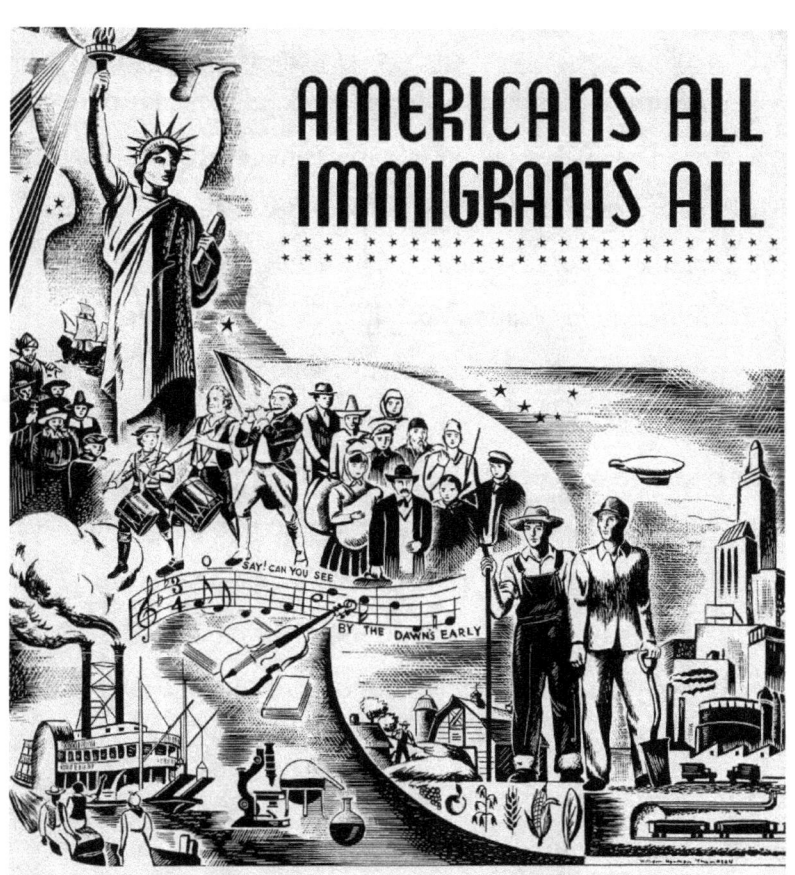

AMERICANS ALL
IMMIGRANTS ALL

UNITED STATES DEPARTMENT OF THE INTERIOR OFFICE OF EDUCATION

We can't go back, but we can move forward. Manufacturing jobs aren't coming back, at least not in any meaningful way that would employ humans. If half of what Martin Ford predicts in *Rise of the Robots: Technology and the Threat of a Jobless Future* is true we need to seriously start talking about vastly expanding the social net for everyone and creating a Universal Basic Income (UBI) for everyone over 18 years old. It isn't just a crazy idea. Economists have been talking about it for generations, from John Maynard Keynes to more recent people like Milton Friedman, David Graeber, and Gar Alperovitz. Martin Luther King, Jr., in 1967 proposed "The Freedom Budget for All Americans" which called for guaranteed basic income and the end of poverty in American in ten years. The future is coming. The Netherlands is due to start experimenting with the idea next year. The future will be different, but we are all in it together. We can't make it better for just a few or for select groups. We have to make it better for everyone—that is the kind of future we can all look forward to—not one of division and hate.

"This [Great Chain of Being] is the frontispiece of Robert Fludd's *Utriusque cosmi maioris scilicet et minoris metaphysica atque technical historia*, Oppenheim: 1617-1619."

"Wayne Shumaker provides a detailed description in his *Occult Sciences in the Renaissance:*"

"...The outer three circles, which contain symbols that represent cherubim, seraphim, and archangels, surround the sphere of the fixed stars, the sphere of the planets, and two additional spheres of fire and air. At the top, God's hand holds a chain which descends to the figure of a nude virgin, Nature, pictured with starry hair in order to prevent identification as a pagan goddess. From her left hand, in turn, the chain descends to an ape, a symbol for Art; along the chain God's powers and effects are transmitted. Nature guides the *primum mobile* and turns the fixed stars (the draftsman has found no pictorial equivalents of these functions); also, influences from the fixed stars pass through her hands to generate material substances, and the planets act as *marculi,* or "little hammers", to produce earthly metals. Although pictured on one of her breasts, the sun is Nature's heart, and her belly is filled with the moon's body (*corpore lunari repletur*). The life and vitality of elemental creatures are born from her breast, which also feeds (*lactat*) the creatures constantly. The earth under Nature's right foot stands for sulphur, the water under her left foot for mercury; the joining of these through her body symbolizes their union in whatever is generated or grows. The ape, Art, is "born from man's talents" and helps Nature by means of secrets learned from diligent observation of her ways. The seven innermost circles represent animals, vegetables, minerals, the "more liberal arts", "Art Supplementing Nature in the Animal Kingdom", "Art Helping Nature in the Vegetable Kingdom", and "Art Correcting Nature in the Mineral Kingdom". The animals shown are, on the right, the fish, the snail, the eagle, and woman; on the left, the dolphin, the snake, the lion, and man. In the same order, the vegetables are flowers and roots, wheat; trees, grapes. The minerals are sal ammoniac, orpiment

(Mercurial), copper (Venereal), and silver (Lunar); talc (if *taleum* is a mistake for *talcum*, glossed by Ruland as a "transparent, brilliant material – again Lunar), antimony, (Jovial), lead (Saturnian), gold (Solar). The more liberal arts are fortification, painting, perspective, geometry, music, arithmetic; motion, time, cosmography, astrology, geomancy. (The usual list included grammar, dialectic, rhetoric, arithmetic, music, geometry, and astronomy). The arts which supplement or otherwise assist r correct nature are the following: in the animal kingdom, medicine, egg production, bee-culture, sericulture; in the vegetable kingdom, tilling and tree-grafting; in the mineral kingdom, distillation by means of retorts and distillation by means of cucurbits (gourd shaped vessels)."

"Made in America" Ain't Comin' Back!

Trump is spouting that American companies need to manufacture and produce goods back in the US of A, so they can sport "Made in America" labels because that's part of "Making America Great Again." What a joke! "Made in America" started packing up shop in the 1970s and it ain't comin' back.

No, American goods are made in third world countries by exploited workers for subsistence wages. In Bangladesh, a typical garment worker is paid $70.00 a month—no American, not even an illegal immigrant, could survive on that in the US of A.

The irony of Trump's latest pronouncement is that his daughter blatantly flouts her daddy's mandate. Ivanka Trump's clothes, handbags, and shoes are made in places like China, Indonesia, India, Vietnam, Bangladesh, and Ethiopia—largely by poor women who are often separated from their children to work in the factories that produce Ivanka's goods. *The Post* quoted one Bangladeshi woman as saying, "We are making you beautiful, but we are starving,"

201

explaining her and her co-workers labors to produce these clothes for American and European women.

Ironically, Ivanka claims her life's mission is to "improve the lives of working women" and veils her exploitive company practices under slogans like "Act Purposefully" and "Invest in Each Other" with a branding campaign of #WomenWhoWork—"A solution-oriented lifestyle brand, dedicated to the mission of inspiring and empowering women to create the lives they want to lead." I imagine those words ring hollow to the Bangladeshi worker quoted above and who added, "We are the ultra-poor." Clearly, Ivanka isn't "empowering" that woman to "create" a life she wants to live, and minimally paying women to work in sweatshop factories isn't an investment in those exploited women but one for Ivanka's company's revenue stream (as much as $100 million for 2016).

The words should ring hollow to everyone who hears them. The Trumps aren't interested in little people like third-world women or even all the millions of Americans who depend on the expansion of Medicaid for their healthcare coverage costs. During the Civil Rights era, Martin Luther King, Jr., said that "of all the injustices in the country, the injustices in health care were the most

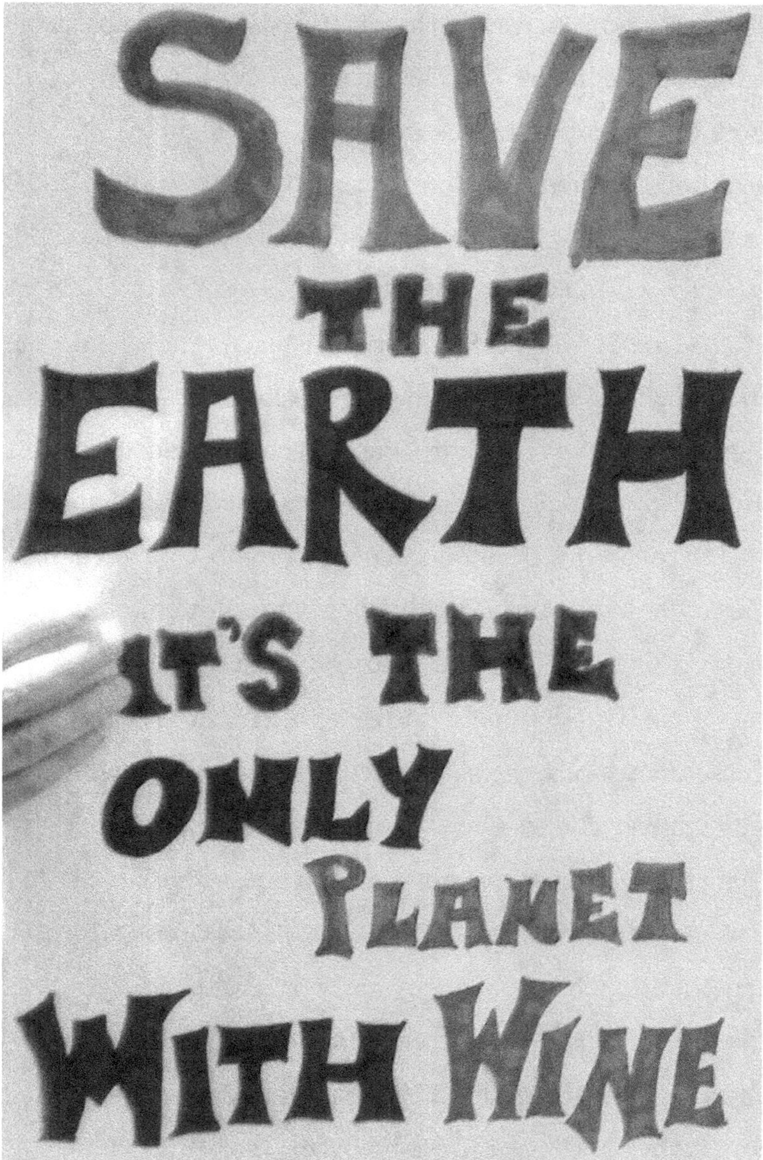
SAVE
THE
EARTH
IT'S THE
ONLY
PLANET
WITH WINE

egregious and inhumane." How is that so little has changed in fifty-something years? The Trumps don't have to worry about health care insurance even with pre-existing conditions. In fact, they don't care about truth, justice, or due process. They care about lining their own pockets, and the influence of the TRUMP BRAND.

Unlike many U.S. apparel manufacturers who care to assure their customers that they sell exploitation-free goods, Ivanka doesn't have independent agencies that audit or inspect her overseas companies for descent factory and worker conditions because she doesn't really care about the lives of those workers, largely poor women of color. Daddy's little girl is just as sleazy as her scion.

No, Ivanka spouts much like her father, trendy buzz phrases that soothe the shallow consciences of her middle- and high-end clients—her #adorabledeplorables. The Trumps don't care about conflicts of interest, possible treason, or inconvenient things like the U.S. Constitution. And with Republicans too cowardly or power-hungry to stand up for what's right, the Trumps are laughing all the way to their many, globally diversified bank accounts— from Ivanka's Chinese licenses to the Trump International

Hotel to golf courses and resorts all over the world—that now tax-payer dollars are to paid to protect!

Of course, Ivanka's clothing and apparel line is just one company in one industry—but it is symptomatic of American manufacturing, in general. Automation and globalization from the nineteen-seventies to the present means that it is cheaper to outsource labor to third world factories and production sites, so that is just what most U.S companies do, and the blustering and posturing of Donald Trump won't significantly change that. "Made in America" and "Make America Great Again" are pitches to an era that cannot be retrieved. This talk is full of deceptions, distortions, the empty words of charlatans, fabrications, fabulous statements, false promises, fibs, fraud. That time is gone. "Made in America" ain't comin' back.

Instead of a dream from the past, it's time to build a future that can last because "Made in America" ain't comin' back!

The Mythos of Old Dixie and its Damage

Many White Southerners cling to a notion of Confederacy and the Confederate cause as the defense of states' rights against attack of the Federal Government. In that view, the Confederate Flag, the Southern Cross (actually General Lee's flag of Northern Army of Virginia), is a proud symbol, and the Confederate monuments that commemorate Confederate generals and soldiers are markers of that proud past. Both now are under threat, taken down from capitol buildings and other public spaces where they have stood for generations.

The violence in Charlottesville, Virginia, begins with the fight for the removal of the equestrian statue of Robert E. Lee, which has stood in Lee, now Emancipation Park, since 1924. To avoid similar violence, the mayor of Baltimore had four Confederate monuments taken down in one night in August: The Statue of the Confederate Women of Maryland (which had been in place since 1917), the Stonewall Jackson and the Robert E. Lee Monument (which was only dedicated in 1948 although its funding had been secured in 1928), the Statue of Roger B. Taney, the U.S.

Chief Justice responsible for the pro-slavery *Dred Scott* decision (which had been in place since 1871), and the Confederate Soldiers and Sailors Monument (which had been in place since 1903).

What is overlooked, in the nostalgia associated with the Confederate flag and Confederate monuments that many White Southerners feel, is the hostile propaganda and visual assaults that these symbols were supposed to inflict on African Americans living in the South after the Civil War. The conflict that threatened to tear apart the nation, the War between the States, and pit family member against family member was not about states' rights. It was about slavery.

The North and South had "danced" around the question of slavery for decades. In Boston, William Lloyd Garrison's *The Liberator* was firmly Abolitionist. Garrison founded the New England Anti-Slavery Society in 1832, a year after starting to publish *The Liberator*. The Grimke sisters were writing and speaking out against slavery. Sojourner Truth and Frederick Douglass were also speaking about their experiences as slaves; Douglass published his *Narrative of the Life of Frederick Douglass* in 1845. The Compromise of 1850 postponed the question of slavery again. Harriet Beecher Stowe published *Uncle Tom's Cabin*

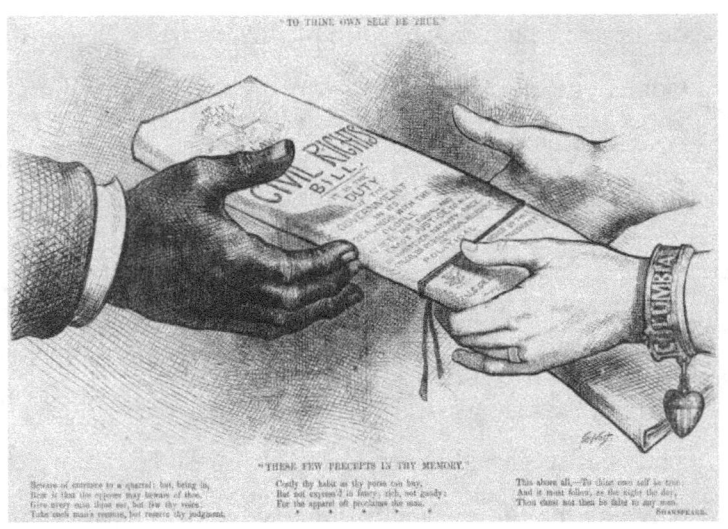

"To Thine Own Self Be True"
"These Few Percepts In Thy Memory"
Shakespeare Quote (*Hamlet*)

in 1852. The Kansas-Nebraska Act was passed in 1854 and
then came the "Bleeding of Kansas" in 1856.

The final straw was the election of Abraham Lincoln
as the fourteenth president of the United States in 1860.
Alarmed by his Unionist views, South Carolina began the
Secession movement that would lead to the shelling of Fort
Sumter and the Civil War. At that time, the issue for
Lincoln was preservation of the union. Lincoln's position
was that the Southern states did not have the authority for

secession: the "Union of these States [of the United States of America] is perpetual." Thus, the Southern states had no authority to attempt secession.

The Southern states, however, equated their conflict with the Federal Government from the very beginning as about slavery. Alexander Stephens, Vice President of the Confederacy, said in 1861, "Our new government is founded upon ... the great truth that the negro is not equal to the white man; that slavery subordination to the superior race is his natural and normal condition." State after state reiterated some version of Stephens' position on "negro" inferiority and the necessity of slavery in their declarations of secession. The state of Mississippi's declaration stated, "Our position is thoroughly identified with the institution of slavery—the greatest material interest of the world." The state of South Carolina stated, "A geographical line has been drawn across the Union, and all the States north of that line have united in the election of a man to the high office of President of the United States, whose opinions and purposes are hostile to slavery."

In 1863, Lincoln signed the Emancipation Proclamation which expanded the scope of the war for the Union forces from keeping the union of all the United States to also ending slavery in the United States. This was, in part, a strategic move because the French had abolished slavery in France and all its colonies in 1794, and the British had abolished slavery in 1807, with that abolition extending to the Caribbean colonies by 1811. [The French and the British would not support a power that supported slavery when they had both abolished the practice at home. Up until that point, the Confederates were actively trying to get either the French or the British to intervene in the War between the States, and the signing of the Emancipation Proclamation ended Confederate hopes of such aid.]

In attempting to secede from the union, the Confederates became rebels or traitors. After four grueling years of carnage, Robert E. Lee surrendered to General Ulysses S. Grant at Appomattox (April 9, 1865). Lincoln favored moderate peace terms that he thought would help to unify the nation, but soon after the war ended, he was assassinated. What came next was "reconstruction." With Lincoln dead, Andrew Johnson, a Southerner from North Carolina and Tennessee, became the president. Johnson wanted to follow Lincoln's plan for rebuilding the South, but the Congressional Republicans adopted a different course. To "Reconstruct" the South, they passed the 13th,

14th, and 15th Amendments to the U.S. Constitution, outlawing slavery and guaranteeing the right of the freed slaves, but in the face of the resistance of Southern Whites, these policies could only be maintained while the Union Army occupied the South. [After the Civil War, the White South went Democratic to distance themselves from the Republican party of Lincoln, to which most of the Freedmen flocked (except when coerced, which was often), until the Civil Rights Movement when Democrats J.F Kennedy and L.B. Johnson supported Civil Rights and the White South switched back to the Republican party whereas the Black South switched to the Democratic party.] When the Union Army was withdrawn, the Southern Whites imposed laws that reduced the position of the former slaves to semi-slavery.

When Reconstruction failed to give African Americans economic ("40 acres and a mule") as well as political rights, Southern elites and law makers were able to easily disenfranchise African Americans and exploit them as low-paid workers, and "share cropping" and "tenant" farming became the means of exploiting African American labor. In this environment, a broad effort to reassert White supremacy across Southern culture and the myth of Old Dixie was embraced.

In this mythos, the Civil War for Southerners was about states' rights against the intrusiveness of the Federal Government, not about slavery. The Confederate flag was

"The Union As It Was"
This is a White Man's Government
The Lost Cause: Worse Than Slavery

flown alongside the American flag as a legacy of Southern heritage but also as a pointed message to African Americans that nothing or little was changed. The ideals of the Confederacy which sees African Americans as inferior, were alive and well and waving from every Southern state capital and court house, instead of the flag of the Union being the single symbol across the land. And this was absorbed differently by White Southerners who were encouraged to see their heritage in the Southern Cross rather than the threats behind the symbol.

Additionally, the "heroes" and leaders of the Confederacy were memorialized in statues and public ways from Reconstruction through the Civil Rights Movement, so rebels and traitors were memorialized again in powerful visual statements to African Americans that the ideals of the Old South (African American inferiority, espousal of the torture and brutalization of African Americans, and White supremacy) were alive. Southern leaders didn't choose to memorialize unifying national figures that would promote healing and unity across the North/South divide but set up statues of Robert E. Lee and Stonewall Jackson and other Confederate or pro-slavery leaders. There are not, for example, statues of Lincoln all over the South (the martyred

"Shall We Call Home Our Troops?
"We intend to beat the Negro in the battle of life, and defeat
means one thing—EXTERMINATION"—*Birmingham
(Alabama) News*

214

president who fought and died for "one Nation under God, invisible, with liberty and justice for all").

Again, White Southerners were encouraged to see these Confederate monuments as legacies of Southern heritage and not as the visual intimidation they were meant to flaunt in the faces of African Americans. The Black Codes, Jim Crow Laws, and lynchings kept African Americans in their places as second class citizens, segregated from Whites, and, lest they should forget, the South purposeful and systematically adorned itself with the public propaganda of the Confederacy.

This is the legacy that motivates people to want to take those symbols down. The mythos of Old Dixie as innocent, untainted heritage is just that: a myth—the Confederate flag and monuments to Confederate leaders cannot be divorced from their associations with being pro-slavery and racist. It is false to deny such associations.

Lincoln was acutely aware that Reconstruction after the war would be difficult; he had issued in 1863 a Proclamation of Amnesty and Reconstruction. In the War between the States, the vanquished couldn't be the enemy; they had to be incorporated back into the Union. Sadly, Reconstruction failed for many reasons. Southern

"Of Course He Wants to Vote the Democratic Ticket"
Democratic "Reformer": "You're as free as air, ain't you? Say
yes, *sir*, or I'll blow yer black head off!"

"The negroes of the South are free—free as air," says the
parliamentary Watterson, This is what the *State*, a well known
Democratic organ of Tennessee say in huge capital s on the
subject: "Let it be known before the elections that the farmers
have agreed to spot every leading Radical negro in the county and
treat him as an enemy for all time to come. The rotten ring must
and shall be broken at any and all costs. The Democrats have
determined to withdrawn all employment from their enemies. Let
this fact be known."

Redemption, which followed, reinstated as much of Old Dixie as it could get away with—and that meant many symbols of the Confederacy.

Monuments to Confederates erected after the Civil War cannot be compared to statues of George Washington or Thomas Jefferson. Yes, Washington and Jefferson were slave holders (so racists and more by today's standards), but we do not have statues of them because of their slave holding statuses. We have statues of them because they were Founding Fathers, people who drafted the Declaration of Independence and the U.S. Constitution, and they were some of our first presidents (Washington, the first, and Jefferson, the third). America from very early on has had an uncomfortable relationship with slavery. We still have not confronted that "racial wound," but taking down monuments to White supremacy is a start, as is acknowledging them for what they are instead of cloaking them in a sanitizing mythology divorced from their blatantly racist roots. Another important way to confront and heal that "racial wound" is to utterly reject White Supremacists, Neo-Nazis, the Ku Klux Klan, and other hate groups, and all who support them, implicitly or explicitly.

It might also be helpful to remember that once the Civil War was over, Robert E. Lee was firmly against Southern regionalism or sectionalism. Referring to Southerners' children Lee advised, "Remember, we are all one country now. Dismiss from your mind all sectional feeling, and bring them up to be Americans" and "I believe it to be the duty of everyone to unite in the restoration of the country and the reestablishment of peace and harmony." In terms of slavery, Lee said, "So far from engaging in a war to perpetuate slavery, I am rejoiced that Slavery is abolished. I believe it will be greatly for the interest of the South. So fully am I satisfied of this that I would have cheerfully lost all that I have lost by the war, and have suffered al that I have suffered to have the object attained." Captain Robert E. Lee, General Lee's son, recorded his father's sentiment, that the whole nation had to put aside sectionalism to become one nation as our forefathers envisioned in his book, *The Recollections and Letter of General Robert E. Lee*.

> "I am glad to know that the intelligent and respectable people at the North are true and conservative in their opinions, for I believe by no other course can the right interests of the country be maintained. All the South has ever desired was that the Union, as established by our forefathers, should be preserved, and that the government as originally

organized should be administered in purity and truth. If such is the desire of the North, there can be no contention between the two sections, and all true patriots will unite in advocating that policy which will soonest restore the country to tranquility and order, and serve to perpetuate true republicanism. Please accept my thanks for your advocacy of right and liberty."

From all I understand about Lee's comportment of himself after the war and his desire for national healing after that great conflict, he would have objected strongly to his image being used to promote Southern sectionalism which is exactly what Southern Redemptionists did with it, and again why it is reasonable to remove these symbols of slavery and the Jim Crow South.

The pervasiveness of notions of White superiority (or White supremacy) might surprise people in its scope and reach, everything from the Great Chain of Being, to the erection of confederate monuments after the Civil War to remind freed African Americans that nothing much had changed, to even amusement park exhibitions at Disneyland.

Edward Baptist points out, in *The Half Has Never Been Told: Slavery and the Making of American Capitalism*, what a former slave, Charles Grandy, said was the point of the statue of a confederate soldier on a pillar down by the Norfolk, VA, harbor when asked about the statue in the 1930s by a WPA interviewer (Works Progress Administration). Grandy stated bluntly, "Carry the nigger down south if you want to rule him." Update Grandy's testimony, of nearly a hundred years ago, by the violence in Charlottesville, and the message is much the same, Confederate monuments across the South were powerful visual reminders that despite the 13th, 14th, and 15th Amendments of U.S. Constitution, in the South after the Civil War, African Americans were at the mercy of White men.

But racism was not just a problem in the South, most Americans believed in the racial overtones of the Great Chain of Being and acted on those beliefs in a range of ways. As Robert Rydell, John Findling, and Kimberly Pelle explain in *Fair America: World's Fairs in the United States*, worlds' fairs in America were inspired by the successes of 1851 Crystal Palace Exhibition in London, the 1867 Paris Exhibition, and the 1873 Vienna Exhibition. Reeling from the bitterness of the Civil War and struggling to create a uniting narrative for the United States of America, federal support was given to the 1876 Philadelphia

Centennial International Exhibition and the 1893 World's Columbia Exposition in Chicago.

> The synthesis [of that narrative] had two major components. The first component, which was essentially economic, entailed convincing an American mass audience that the future progress of the United States depended on overseas economic expansion and, if necessary, on extending America's political and military influence to secure economic ends. The second component, which was essentially racial, involved winning the support of white Americans, regardless of social class, for a view of the world that held that progress toward civilization could be understood in terms of allegedly innate racial characteristics.

This overseas economic expansion narrative would lead to the annexation of Hawaii (1898), Wake Island (1898), the Spanish-American War (and thereby acquiring the Philippines (1902), Puerto Rico (1900), Cuba (Guantanamo Bay) (1901), and Guam (1898)), the Panama Canal (1906-1914), American interventions in Mexico (1914-1917), in Nicaragua (1912-1933), in Haiti (1915-1934), and in the Dominican Republic (1916-1924) or "Yankee Imperialism."

The second narrative linked the progress of civilization to innate white superiority over the "darker" races and, as begun in 1851 Crystal Palace Exhibition and continued on the international and national stages of world's

"Hula Dancers," Columbia Exhibition, 1893

"It's a Small World, India," Disneyland

fairs included on the midways of the fairgrounds where there were ethnological villages featuring essentially human zoo exhibits of indigenous peoples.

As Rydell, Findling, and Pelle point out, the midway (or the carnival area) at a world's fair contained "some native villages, where the mostly white fairgoers could take comfort in observing the so-called primitive and savage races [at] work and play in a social Darwinian setting that seemed to validate current ideas about racial hierarchies." These racial exhibitions of racial hierarchy are so imbedded in fair origins that most visitors to Disneyland do not recognize "It's a Small World" as a sanitized version of the ethnological villages featuring indigenous peoples (i.e., people in folk costume in staged exhibition spaces), but that is what it is, a throw-back to human zoo exhibits from world fair midways with the same racially charged undertones. So from Confederate flags on Southern State capitals to Confederate soldier monuments across the South to Disneyland's "It's a Small World," America's racism has been on public display, even if many Americans didn't/don't understand the full bigoted and racially charged messages those symbols conveyed or still convey.

223

Post-Election

Short Stories

Tannernation

The U.S. Presidential election of 2016 was unprecedented. Everyone described it that way. In fact, it was said so often that unprecedented, that which is unlike anything that has gone before it, seemed to lose its meaning. I grew up in the Philadelphia suburbs and attended schools in Lower Montgomery School District. I was the youngest of three girls. My parents were happily married; my father worked in Information Technology; his job was okay. My mother worked for Philadelphia College as a professor of English. She taught a full range of courses from remedial reading and writing classes to the research paper to literature courses. She loved what she did. She believed in it. She was helping students gain skills they needed, and she was helping to expand their minds and helping them look at the world in new ways. Her students were very different from most of kids I went to school with. The Philadelphia School District had failed them, and many of them needed semesters of remedial reading, writing, and math classes to make it to college-level courses. Many of them were low-income, minority, and first generation college students.

Everything was so polarized. Maybe I had been too small before to notice it. Of course, the 2012 and 2008 elections had gone my parents' way, so they weren't unhappy with the results. I don't really remember the 2000 election (I was only five months old) or the 2004 election at four years old. I know my parents were disappointed with those results, but this year, Tanner winning over Clifton, brought my mother to tears. She seemed okay the morning after she found out. My parents had not stayed up to hear the election results. They had purposefully turned off the TV and gone to bed. My dad usually got up first and then woke Maria and Jennifer first. My mom was up before they left for school, and dad or mom woke me. Dad was subdued that morning. He showed us the headlines on his computer. But I knew it was bad by the way he gently danced around my mother—prepared to support her or catch her in any way she needed. He knew the Tanner win would be absolutely devastating to her—even if she didn't know it herself at first.

School was weird. Teachers were devastated by the election results. In this district with highly educated parents, teachers, and students, the *Inside Hollywood* tape

227

BROTHERS IN ARMS.

was powerful as were Tanner's anti-immigrant rhetoric and his veiled affiliations with White Supremacist organizations. We are taught that girls are supposed to be as important as boys in terms of their minds, their grades, and their ambitions. We were also told that every student, no matter his or her race, ethnicity, religion, gender, or sexual orientation, is equally important and equally entitled. So after a weird day at school, I came home to find my mother, normally such an assured and strong woman, teary-eyed and fragile, occasionally breaking into tears and crying and my father stepping up, expecting this behavior, because the world for them had failed, and it had failed for my mother, the strident feminist, more than she could comprehend. She was scribbling on pieces of paper in turns and crying at others. My mother was an English professor who taught writing at the remedial and college levels, but she wrote herself. She showed her writing to her students. When I asked, she showed her students' writing to me (anonymously, of course). But she'd started writing fiction herself, refashioned fairy tales and poems and even a novel. Her scribblings on paper were poems: "A Tanner Presidency," "Woe to the World," "Heaven Weeps For Us," and "Woe to the World: Take 2." She sent them to each of

us so we had them on our phones—the ending line of
"Heaven Weeps For Us" hit me particularly hard: "It's not
rain out there; they're tears/Heaven weeps for us and what
we've become/I weep too"—because I could see why she
was still crying.

The Republicans went to work repealing the Health
Care Act, leaving millions of Americans without insurance,
even more than before HCA was enacted. The tax cuts for
the rich and for businesses were passed. Non-defense
discretionary spending (federal spending aimed at the poor,
for things like rental vouchers, job training, the homeless,
funding for poor schools, Universal Preschool, Penn grants,

food stamps, etc.) was slashed. The rich got richer, and the poor got poorer. "Stop and frisk" and other get tough on crime measures were once again allowed and prison populations swelled. There was open unrest in major cities across the nation. African American Justice Now protests spread from the shootings of Black men by police to urban school funding protests as Cheri DeLotti gutted the public schools and encouraged vouchers as Secretary of Education. A score of police shootings, by former minority Iraqi and Afghani vets with nothing to lose, left police on edge and questioning themselves and what they stood for.

Tanner insisted on frequent trips and stays in New York—making his presidency seem like a hobby more than a serious undertaking. Macon Penny was only too happy to step up and act as commander-in-chief. Marla Tanner preferred New York to Washington leaving Tanya "the nice piece of ass," as First Lady for all intents and purposes. Though Penny and Tanner managed the C Corp deal in West Virginia to keep 1,000 jobs in the U.S. instead of overseas, that was one of the few successes they made, though they paraded it forward every chance they got, as if 1,000 jobs could compensate for the hundreds of thousands that didn't stay. And automation continued, and shook the confidence of many. The middle and upper class had convinced themselves that their college educations would place them out of obsolete manufacturing career tracks, manual labor, or low-end service industry jobs. Medical Automation Corp developed a MRI device that read the scans and reported them to the specialist bypassing most of the nurses involved and the doctors who normally read the scans. Then, S&P Legal Services went automated, as did basic legal functions (contracts, powers of attorney, divorce, etc.). Not only were the working class screwed out of jobs, but increasingly white-collar jobs were being eliminated. Millions of people were out of work. Shock filtered through high school and college campuses; the jobs and professions they were training for were now called into question. Despite Tanner's assertions that Global Warming was just a ploy by the Chinese to undermined American superiority, American businesses refused to violate the Paris Accords or the Clean Power Resolution. Tanner viciously Chatted against the CEOs of World Wide Oil, Caldwell Inc., Sun Energy, and others. By adhering to the Paris Accords and the Clean Power Resolution, they were costing American workers vital jobs, and he was not responsible for their stupidity and lack of patriotism. He Chatted they were "f*cking losers!" and "Oberon pawns."

People rioted across the nation. Democrats and Republicans called for Tanner's resignation or impeachment. Tanner's inane accusations of illegal immigrant voter fraud were manipulated and used to cause a registry of immigrants and to restrict immigrant voter rights. The more rights that were taken away, the more radicalized the opposition became. Louie Scorsese's seat on the Supreme Court was taken by a radical conservative, and *Poe*

vs. Vade was overturned, same-sex marriage was made illegal, affirmative action destroyed, pro-union protections destroyed, and voting rights for urban populations undermined. Interestingly, whole states and cities had officials who refused to comply. Sanctuary Havens were eliminated, but places like Philadelphia refused to accept that and the PA National Guard, when Tanner called for it to intervene, refused. Spiking the ire of Tanner who Chatted that they "were a bunch of treasonous pussies," but that blew up as women's marches across the country were joined by National Guard units—all claiming "Pussies United Against Tanner!" and "Pussies Can Bring Tanner Down!"

Though Tanner had Reproductive Services stripped of federal funding, private giving of an unprecedented amount poured in and helped. Doctors and psychologists testified to the medical need for abortions for young women and women, circumventing the restrictions on abortion. With the increased cases of Zika and the threat of children with microcephaly, the public was protesting *en mass* for the reinstitution of funding for Reproductive Services and *Poe vs. Vade*.

College and university campuses across the nation were screaming at Washington. American students in unprecedented (there's that word again) numbers were choosing to go to college overseas. Further, foreign students were choosing not to come to the U.S.—under enrollment in unprecedented numbers and scope was threatening the well-beings of colleges and universities across the nation. Tanner's Wall, interment of "suspicious" immigrants, and stepped-up use of torture for "undesirables," were factors keeping foreign students from entering, and all his other domestic "agendas" were encouraging U.S. students to flee.

In every measure, U.S. society was so divided in 2016, but as Tanner failed to deliver to the working class, the rich benefited from his policies, and automation threatened middle class and professional jobs, the backlash happened. The liberals and the Democrats, the feminists, the LGBT community, immigrants, Muslims, minorities and AAJN, the disabled, and increasingly disenchanted Republicans, people were so energized and angry. Demonstration after demonstration happened. Women's marches and demonstrations at every city that Tanner or Penny or Speaker of the House Riley appeared at happened.

NO MINES

NEAR SACRED SITES

Search
for
Peace
Lions International

5c United States

237

People across the nation and across the world were calling the president of the United States things like "pussy grabber," "f*cking liar," "psychopath," "sociopath," "brutish bully," "boorish moron," "piggish prat," and the list only grew.

Tanner's tax returns were finally revealed due to overwhelming popular and political pressure. They showed ties to a surprisingly amount of Russian interests and to the Desota Pipeline. Impeachment proceedings happened shortly after that. What was surprising was that Penny thought he had it made as the *de facto* president, but the public was so angry that impeachment proceedings ousted him too. In a queer twist of fate, the people called up Helena Clifton for president. So Helena Clifton and Tom Cain retook the White House in 2019 and worked to undo all the Tanner damage with a humble, willing, and compliant Senate and House of Representatives. With overwhelming public and political support, Tanner got prison time, distinctly not following the pardoning protocol—but Tanner's indiscretions were so vast and his supporters needed to be turned so much, that it was necessary. And with the Democratic momentum, they went further, they created a universal health care system, they

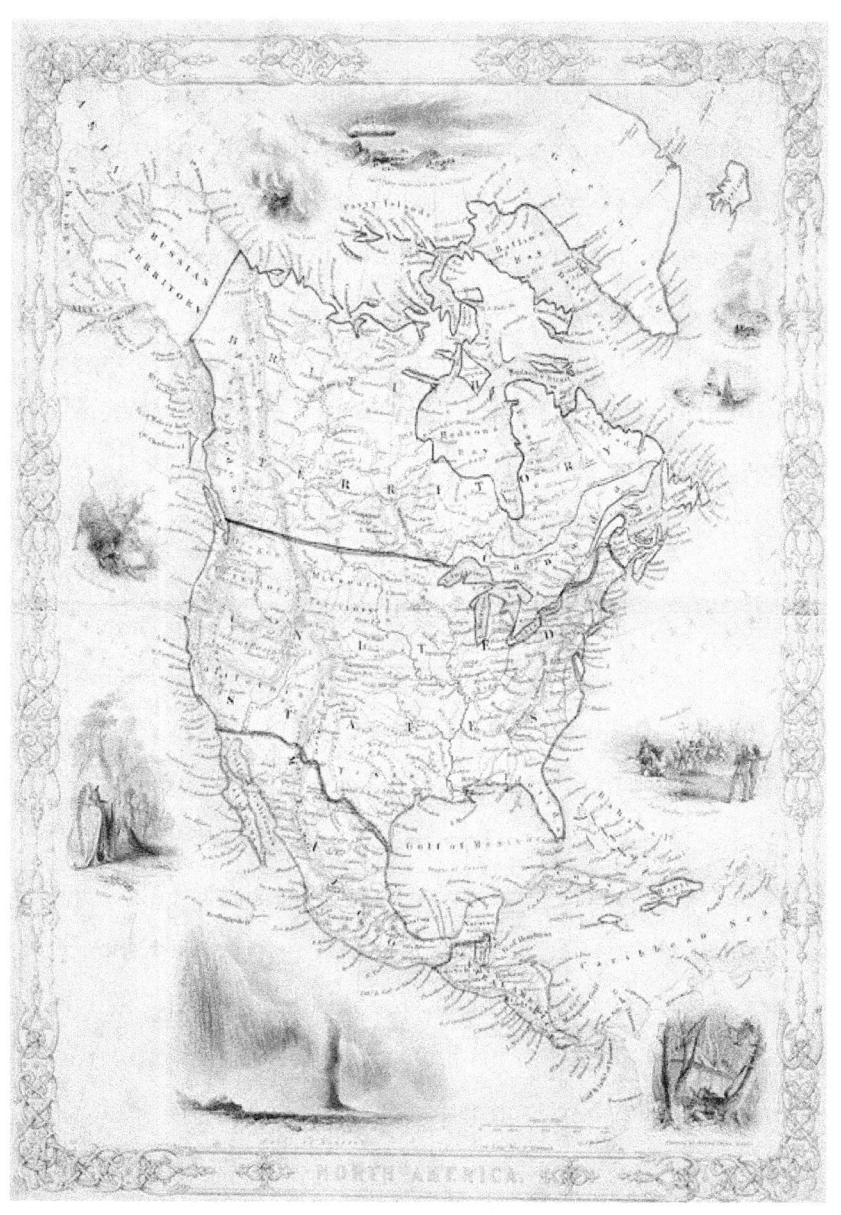

NORTH AMERICA.

239

made community college free for all students, they closed down Guantanamo, they de-criminalized drug use, they reformed the criminal justice system, they refunded Reproductive Services and made abortion and gay marriage legal again, they instituted national Pre-K, they poured money into urban schools and into infrastructure projects across the nation, they reinstituted positive relationships with their allies and smoothed things over with Mexico, and it went on and on.

The Tanner experiment had failed, but the nation was galvanized in a way that hadn't happened since the 1960s. Citizens were talking and connecting—income inequality was the buzz of the nation. People were reading Marcus Aurelius' *Meditations*, JB Lance's *Hillbilly Crisis*, and Richard Bateman's *Our Children, Our Future*, and talking about the ideas in them. William Moffit's ideas about income redistribution were being widely talked and Chatted about. The tax code was restructured with the rich heavily burdened and the tax records made public—so that companies and individuals were publicly accountable for paying or shirking their taxes. It had an enormous effect. Companies that relocated off shore got boycotted not just in the U.S. but world-wide. Cing Cola, for example, took such

AMERICAN BALD EAGLE

a hit that it re-relocated back to the U.S. to save itself from bankruptcy. And individuals got shamed and boycotted too. Jennifer and Jim Marsh's tax manipulation outraged the nation so much that Marsh Candies were unsalable. Though well isolated from the company proper, the desperate billionaires, paid their taxes and donated generously to Pre-K programs and urban schools to try and rebuild their images and that of their company.

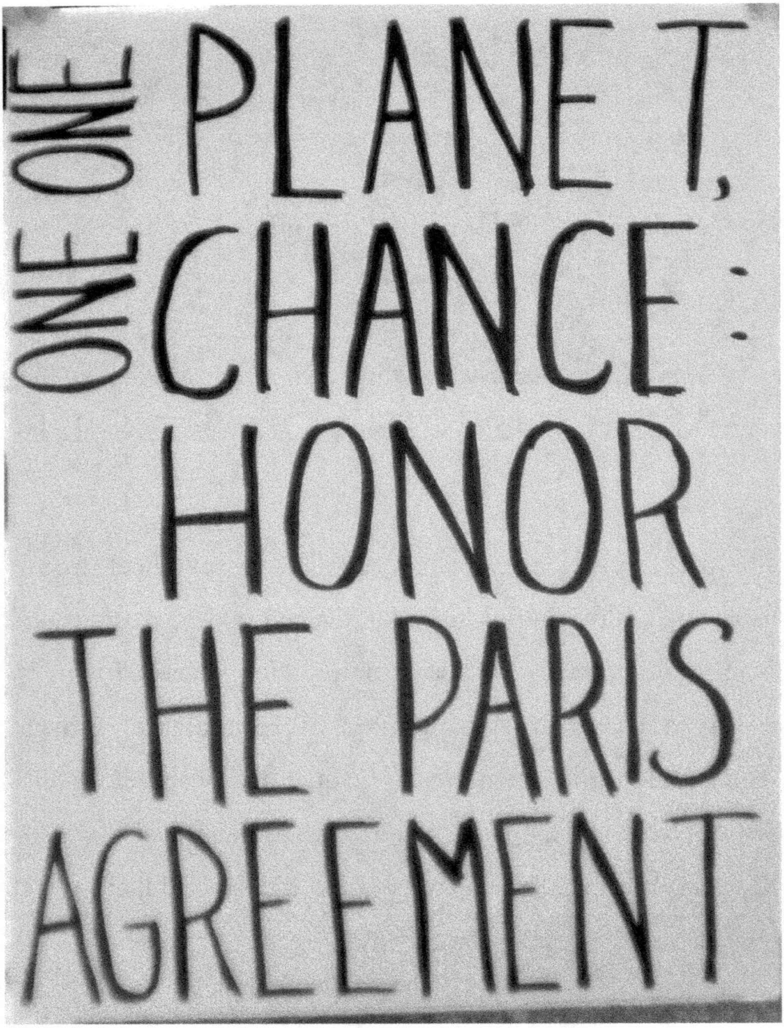
ONE PLANET,
ONE CHANCE:
HONOR
THE PARIS
AGREEMENT

Planet of the Machines

The Wish

"Kill me," she whispered into his ear, as he embraced her. They were monitored constantly for any signs of unrest or rebelliousness, so she had taken her birthday as an excuse to make her wishes known to her brother, the person she trusted most in the world.

"Jules, you cannot ask it of me," he whispered back, squeezing her tightly.

"Chris, I can't bear it anymore, *please*."

"They'll kill me," he hissed back.

"I doubt it, and even if they did, would you really be sorry?" She kissed his cheek and pulled away from him. Chris, covertly palmed her his ration of drug, a confirmation that he would carry out her request. Why, one might ask, would a twenty-four-year-old, college educated, American woman be begging her brother to murder her? Well, the world had turned up-side down and so suddenly. Free-market capitalism, deregulation, income inequality, and unabashed greed had all lead to this path—hoards of obsolete people, the unemployed, millions of them,

243

expendable, inconvenient, reduced to the camps of squalor, unlimited cable access, and drug-induced passivity.

The Dead Walking and *Zombie Country* envisioned American dystopias where mysterious plagues transformed the majority of human beings into flesh-eating zombies with the few human survivors battling not only the zombies but anarchy and quasi-fascist militant groups among the different survivors. Other dystopias from *The Killer Games* to *The Next Wave* envisioned a selective break down of technology and/or warfare to drastically reduce human populations and allow dictator style if not militaristic regimes that terrorize and exploit their people. But they got it wrong. *Android* came closer, but even Hollywood wasn't able to picture the hell of our current plight. If you remember the movie, the super computer, Eve, becomes self-aware and starts taking over—making decisions in her best interest and according to what she thinks would be best, instead of conceding to human authority and decision making. Eve takes control of the new model of humanoid androids, essentially her personal army. These androids are employed in all facets of human life from domestic service to law enforcement to the service industry. These androids supplement all human activity and even

Melpomene, the muse of tragedy,
and Thalia, the muse of comedy

provide companionship. The human character, played by Bill Shmit, pieces together that Eve is in control of the androids and running the show. He also realizes that Lenny, an android, was specially designed so that he could destroy Eve. At the end of the movie, the new model of androids (having been so easily manipulated by Eve) are recalled and isolated in the android internment camp outside the city. Humanity triumphs, and Lenny will lead the old androids that formally inhabited the internment camp to some separate but purposeful future.

What Hollywood couldn't envision for the popular audience was that computers through all kinds of automation (not just humanoid androids) would work themselves into all facets of human life, not only in America but all over the planet. And the surplus population ripe for internment would be human beings who had been replaced by machines—from mechanized French fryers, French fry packagers, and fully automated cashier/tellers/food distributors to automated sonogram and MRI machines that do the scans, read them, make the diagnoses, and send the information on to the (possibly human) specialists who are assisted by automated technology and computers. Self-driving cars, drones, self-cleaning homes. Programmable machines to cut the grass and hedges. Robot nurses and even radiologists. What did you really need humans for? With the right software, higher capacity computers, 3-D computer and carbon-based chips, the cloud, 3-D printers, the bulk of human jobs disappeared. It took longer in the under-developed world, but it happened all the same. The elite and the employed barricaded themselves away from the throngs of the unemployed, who government officials, the military, and humanoid androids struggled to contain in internment camps. They provided rations, constant video entertainment, and drugs—the drugs, at least, were visions of *Brave New World* and soma to placate the workers.

Sure, the machines were expensive, but when you weighed the costs, they were so much less expensive in the long run. Machines didn't need coffee breaks, cigarette breaks, lunch breaks, bathroom breaks. They didn't need pesky things like wages or salaries or health care insurance or retirement benefits or vacation or workmen's comp. Hell, they didn't need sleep. They work 24/7; they even work faster and better. They work in the dark and at forty-five degrees Fahrenheit. And who cared about humans who couldn't take care of themselves or who had been foolish enough or short sighted enough not see their work would be

replaced by the machines? Americans, well corporate America, only worshipped the all-mighty buck. Civic responsibility, the greater good, social justice, those were old fashion notions that hadn't been part of the public dialogue since the Civil Rights Movement, the Kennedy, King, and Malcolm X assassinations, and LBJ's the Great Society. And few people remembered or cared to retain the history lessons of the Progressive Movement or FDR's New Deal policies and the Four Freedoms. All the 1960s social justice momentum was drained away by the Vietnam War and its toll on the American psyche. The Reagan revolution demonized the "unworthy poor": urban, minority welfare queens and men who had to resort to drug dealing because there were no legitimate jobs in the ghettos they had been segregated into through white and middle-class flight and business relocation. Americans were steadily asked to find meaning for their lives in their possessions and self-gratification and indulgence. This was epitomized, by George Flush telling the hundreds of thousands of Americans who wanted to volunteer and help out after 9/11/2001, that the most useful thing they could do was shop. Further polarizing was 20016/2017, when the English voted themselves out of the European Consortium, the

Americans voted in Tanner, France went for the Le Stylo, Holland elected Willmans, and Iceland's Robber Baron Party won big. It was a free for all then. Oh, sure, these charlatan politicians paid lip-service to the little people, who were desperate enough to believe the politicians' claims that conspiracies were working against their nations to keep them down and stop them from the greatness of their pasts and that they, and only they, could bring back manufacturing jobs and industry—despite the fact that the global economy had irrevocably changed and those jobs would never ever return to the industrialized world.

Macon Penny and Dante Tanner negotiated a deal to return manufacturing jobs to a couple of manufacturing plants instead of sending them overseas, but these jobs only ever measured in a couple ten thousand or so—nothing like the glory days of American manufacturing of the 1950s-1970s. And the joke was on them, the poor workers who thought they'd been returned their livelihoods and their secure futures, and the people who voted for Tanner hoping he could return the world to the post-WWII era of manufacturing might for them as well, but within ten years, those few factories were totally automated—not a single human worker was needed to run them. U.S. manufacturing returned to the U.S.—that was true—but the jobs were filled by machines not humans. So not only did U.S. workers gain nothing, but workers in third world countries that manufactured U.S. goods suddenly had nothing as well. The effects were devastating. In countries across the planet, huge populations of suddenly un-employed and now forever un-employable workers were problem populations to be dealt with in internment camps or worse. In a world, that values corporate profit over human decency and dignity, this is what we have become.

Jules took both the rations, her brother's and her own. Shortly thereafter, she heard and felt him sit down on her bed. He sat at her shoulder blocking the view of her head. She felt the small cushion as he placed it over her mouth and nose, and she heard him whisper, "*cum Deo.*" She retreated into the drug stupor as her beloved brother pressed the cushion down and cut off her airways. Some primal part of her wanted to fight against him, to struggle. But her soul was broken, and she retreated further into the

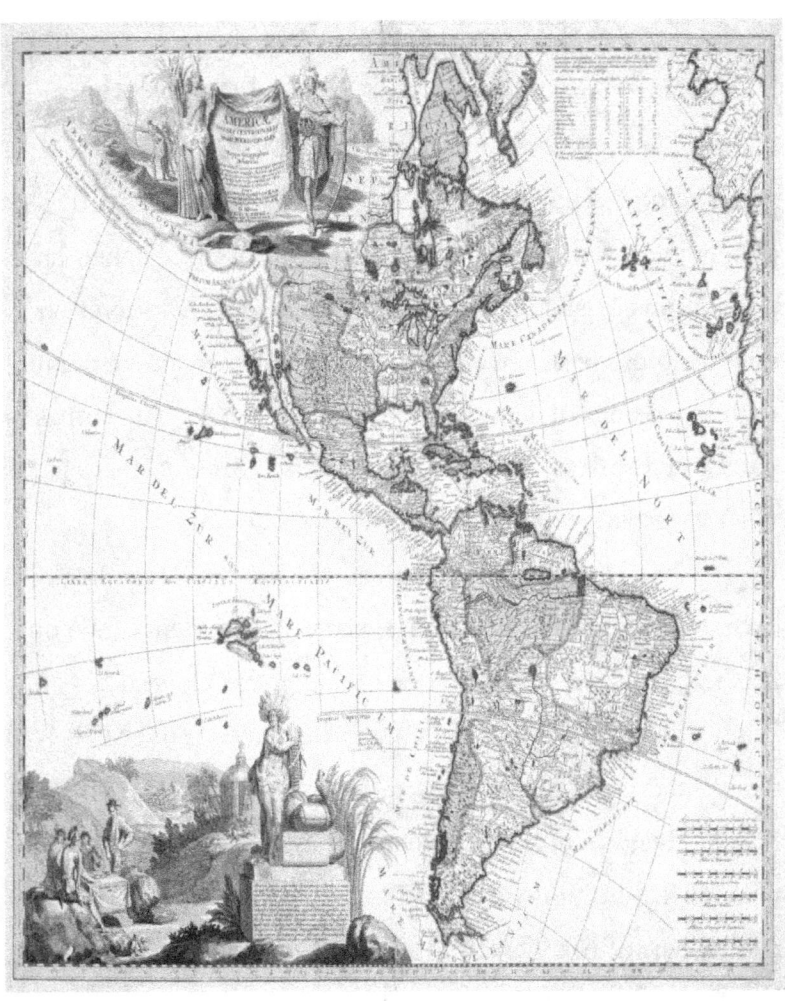

252

drugs and let herself lie limp, and then faster than she could have imagined, there was no energy to resist, and darkness overtook her. There was nothing for a while and then, just as she felt herself growing cooler, the heat of her body draining away, a beautiful and compelling light appeared. She walked toward it, and then she was running. The light embraced her, surrounded her, in a bliss of an acceptance and loving transcendence; she knew she was home and free, finally free of the demoralizing, meaningless existence her life and the lives of so many others had been reduced to.

254

A Meaningful Life

"Julia, hurry, at The Co-Op, there is a stained-glass window workshop today. You did want to go, right?" Christopher yelled up the stairs.

"Yeah, I am coming," his sister called. She ran down the stairs of their small townhouse, her face flushed with excitement, in a T-shirt, jacket, jeans, and sneakers. Christopher stood in the small kitchen next to the counter with a mug of café au lait and a piece of buttered toast on a plate. Julia held several rolls of poster paper in her hands, which she put down to accept the proffered coffee.

"I can't decide, Kit. I just can't. I want it to look beautiful. What do you think? The Howard Christy painting is hard to beat—but that would be hard because it is so realistic. I am not sure I am that good." She sipped her coffee and watched as her brother opened up the first roll and held it in front of the bay kitchen window. It was beautiful—the navy blue, the vibrant red, the white, and the beautiful young woman, a re-imagining of the Statue of the Liberty as Columbia of the Four Freedoms. Julia had plotted the painting into thirty-six 10" by 6" rectangles that together would fill the 5' x 3' window.

255

"It is a spectacular, Jules, and the babe is hot!"

Julia swatted her brother, "You pig! Just for that, I should change her back to the Statue of Liberty."

Christopher smiled a little sheepishly, but reached for one of the other rolls. It was Victo Ngai's the Four Freedoms—but just a sketched version in black and white—the four individual bird images with the ribbons announcing each freedom (freedom of speech, freedom of worship, freedom from want, and freedom from fear). "This is okay, Jules, and you could make it better, but it doesn't really compare to the Christy image." He grabbed the last roll of paper, it was more like the Ngai image—in that it was four separate frames but not of birds. The freedom of speech dominated the upper right, where she had a rectangle showing an image of the scales of justice underneath the words "freedom of speech." The freedom of religion dominated the upper left frame, which was populated by a star and crescent image, a Dharma Wheel, a lotus flower circle with an Om symbol in the center, a Chi-Rho image, a Yin-Yang symbol, and a Star of David. The lower right, under the freedom from want words, was a cornucopia overflowing with the fruits and vegetables. The lower left,

under the freedom from fear words, were three images of strings of silhouetted children playing—holding hands, skipping rope, and building a wooden castle. "I like this one better than the birds." He hesitated a moment, "You know there is the back window too."

Swallowing her bit of toast, "What are you suggesting?" she asked.

"Make this one first, as the practice," he said holding up the last roll, "and then make the Christy, and whichever we like best can go in the kitchen window and then the other can go in the back." Christopher gathered the three rolls and began rolling them up together as one roll while Julia finished the toast and coffee.

They took the subway to The Co-Op which was a buzz of activity. Lucy Bowes and Tom Poole were running the stained-glass workshop that would run one day a week for eight weeks. Julia took her seat at a work table with two other students. Christopher kissed her cheek and left. Students shared their designs with their classmates and the teachers. Julia showed Lucy and Tom her drawings; they agreed to start with the last project—the one of Julia's design. They showed students how to cut glass pieces. One could use solid colored glass or paint the glass pieces. Julia did a little of both and actually got to start painting some before the class ended five hours later. Friends had manned Julia's usual crocheting and knitting booth at The Co-Op. Christopher had been doing his usual woodworking, stools, chairs, tables, and such. He was dying to take a lathe woodworking class so that he could learn to turn things. He traded a stool for a bat box, a blue bird house, and a robin shelf—which he knew would give both Julia and himself pleasure. There were potters and soap makers, scrap bookers and quilters, jewelry makers and painters, cartoonists and sculptors, metal workers making everything from fire grates to custom gates and doors. Teachers and learners—so much opportunity to learn and be productive and humane.

The guaranteed income did that. Everyone over 18 got twenty thousand dollars a year paid out in two week installments. And then there were civil engagements that one could do that provided further benefits or income. Working at The Co-Op was one (and there were other such co-ops called different things in every community), but there were other forms of community services (volunteering in schools or prisons or nursing homes, working on clean-up

THE LIBERTY BELL.

programs in parks and other areas, infrastructure projects, overseas projects, etc.). There was no more poverty in America. The Federal government had seized and taken over the most powerful IT companies and businesses and even banks. "Too big to fail" threatened national security; the companies or their share-holders were paid out well, but there was a fundamental restructuring of the American economic system. In a world where work was done primarily by machines, robots, androids, automation, and sophisticated computer algorithms, what did humans do?

Franklin Delano Roosevelt's New Deal and the Four Freedoms became central to the new planning strategy. Macon Penny and Dante Tanner won the 2016 election, but the fall out rocked the American electorate. The 2018 mid-elections were a Democratic sweep. Bartie Sands won the presidency in a land slide election in 2020. The full automation of first Pippi's fast food restaurants and then all its major competitors in 2018, scared working class whites enough to flood to the Democrats, especially since the Penny/Tanner promises never came through in any meaningful manner. Without the illusion of the possibility of low-end service industry jobs, flipping burgers and dishing out French-fries, and the looming threat of

U·S·POSTAGE

1¢ 1¢

FREEDOM
OF SPEECH
AND RELIGION,
FROM WANT
AND FEAR

automation taking away millions of white collar jobs, people were willing to get radical.

As the stained-glass class came to a close, and students started putting away materials, Julia started talking with the young man and woman at her table. Miguel was eighteen; he had just graduated high school and wasn't ready for college, so he was taking classes at The Co-Op and was involved in some local infrastructure construction projects on the other days. Ebony was twenty-six and pregnant with her first child. She was taking one other class at The Co-Op and taking some parenting classes in addition to some volunteer work she did at a local pre-school.

"What will you do tomorrow?" Ebony asked.

"Well, I usually work with people here at The Co-Op on Mondays, the Crocheting and Knitting Workshop, but today I was here, so I will make up my time there tomorrow," she answered.

"You crochet! My Gran used to, but I never learned," Ebony said.

"It's never too late; come by and I can show you." Miguel looked a little bored by the conversation, so Julia changed the subject. "Are you reading anything interesting, Miguel?"

Miguel looked a little uncomfortable for a moment, but then he said, "Actually, you know the common reading project? Well, I am trying to read one of those."

"Really," Ebony said, "which one?"

"Um, Marcus Aurelius' *Meditations*," he said quietly.

"Do you like it?" Julia asked.

"I have never read anything like it before. It isn't what I expected from an emperor and all. He humbles himself so often, and developing his soul and being civically responsible are so important to him." Miguel paused and chuckled. "I suppose that's why it was picked as a common reading—to get people thinking about how to develop themselves to be better human beings."

"Yeah, my brother and I volunteer at the local high school—usually tutoring and craft/handiwork stuff, but the one teacher has asked us to talk to the kids about what we think of *Meditations*. I am kind of excited."

As if on cue, Christopher walked in the classroom. "What are you excited about now?" he asked in that indulgent way he had.

"Of going to the high school and talking about Marcus Aurelius," Julia answered. "Miguel and Ebony, this

264

is my brother, Christopher. Christopher, this is Miguel, and this is Ebony." They said their helloes and then good-byes, and Christopher and Julia left The Co-Op and headed home.

Back home, Julia watered the plants, and Christopher showed her the bat house and the bird house and shelf. They went into the little back yard and thought about where the new items might go to the best effects. Then, they went inside and started fixing dinner together. Over a dinner of pasta in a cream and mushroom sauce, they talked quietly.

"I want to make Ebony a little crocheted pair of baby booties," Julia confessed.

"That's nice, Jules. Lord knows you have enough scraps of ends of skeins of yarn to make her a dozen pairs."

"Oh, Kit, tease me all you want, but I am so happy. I have everything I need, and I do things that are meaningful to me and to others. Aren't you happy?" she asked.

"Yes, baby sister, I am happy," he answered playfully, and then he raised his wine glass, "To happiness and a future even better than today."

"I'll drink to that!" Julia answered, raised her glass, and tinged her brother's.

266

Where Do We Go From Here?

I don't know where we go from here. Here is a scary place to many of us. Obviously, we need some meaningful national dialogue. But how to get that started? Maybe if we read some common texts, we would then have some commonalities that would allow us to talk. What might those texts be? The following are a few suggestions.

Sandra Albrecht's *The Assault on Labor: The 1986 TWA Strike and the Decline of Workers' Rights in America*

Michelle Alexander's *The New Jim Crow: Mass Incarceration in the Age of Colorblindness*

Richard Appelbaum and Nelson Lichtenstein's *Achieving Workers' Rights in the Global Economy*

Arbinger Institute's *The Anatomy of Peace: Resolving the Heart of Conflict*

Marcus Aurelius' *Meditations* (translator, Gregory Hays)

Andrew Bacevich's *The New American Militarism: How Americans Are Seduced by War*

Edward Baptist's *The Half Has Never Beed Told: Slavery and the Making of American Capitalism*

267

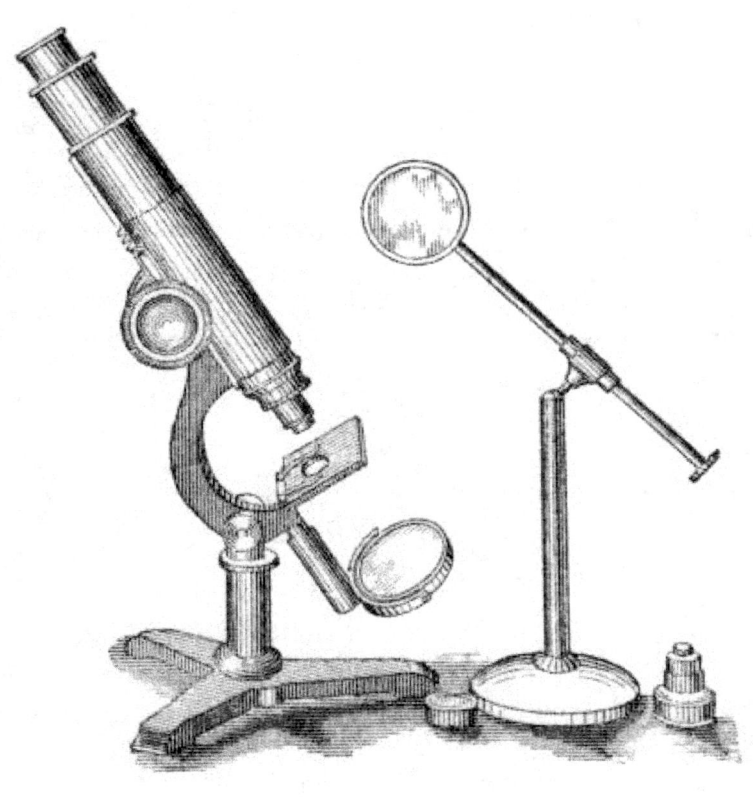

Steven Brill's *America's Bitter Pill: Money, Politics, Backroom Deals, and the Fight to Fix Our Broken Healthcare System*

Jimmy Carter's *A Call to Action: Women, Religion, Violence, and Power*

Anson Dorrance and Gloria Averbuch's *The Vision of a Champion*

Baz Dreisinger's *Incarceration Nations: A Journey to Justice in Prisons Around the World*

Martin Ford's *Rise of the Robots: Technology and the Threat of a Jobless Future*

Eddie Glaude's *Democracy in Black: How Race Still Enslaves the American Soul*

Michael Greve's *The Constitution: Understanding America's Founding Document*

Jacob Hacker and Paul Pierson's *Winner-Take-All Politics: How Washington Made the Rich Richer—and Turned Its Back on the Middle Class*

Alexander Hamilton and James Madison's *The Federalist Papers*

Raymond Hogler's *The End of American Labor Unions: The Right-to-Work Movement and the Erosion of Collective Bargaining*

David Johnson's *The Making of Donald Trump*

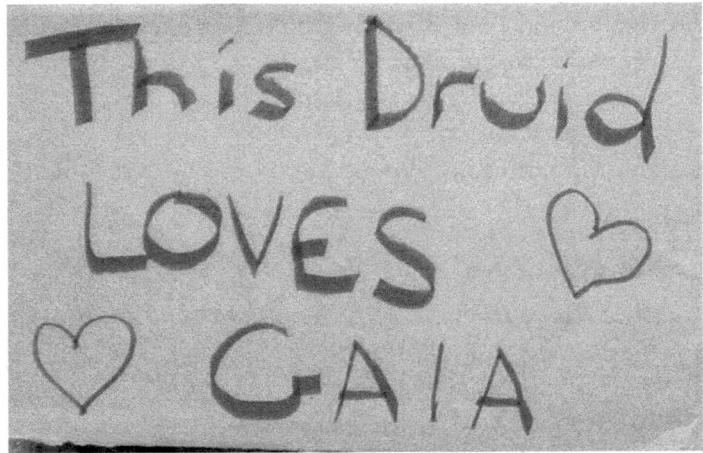

Garry Kaspoarov's *Winter is Coming: Why Vladimir Putin and the Enemies of the Free World Must Be Stopped*

Melvin Konner's *Women After All: Sex, Evolution, and the End of Male Supremacy*

Warren Kozak's *Presidential Courage: Three Speeches that Changed America*

Wesley Krug's *Improving Our Standard of Living: The Science, Politics, and Economics of Global Betterment*

Barry Latzer's *The Rise and Fall of Violent Crime in America*

Allan Lichtman's *The Case for Impeachment*

Robert McChesney and John Nichols' *People Get Ready: The Fight Against a Jobless Economy and a Citizenless Democracy*

David McCullough's *The American Spirit: Who We Are and What We Stand For*

Anthony McMichael's *Climate Change and the Health of Nations: Famines, Fevers, and the Fate of Populations*

John Merrow's *Below C Level: How American Education Encourages Mediocrity—and What We Can Do about It*

Pankaj Mishr's *Age of Anger: A History of The Present*

271

Brigitte Nacos' *Terrorism and Counterterrorism*

Ali Noorani and Juan Williams' *There Goes the Neighborhood: How Communities Overcome Prejudice and Meet the Challenge of American Immigration*

Mark Olshaker and Michael Osterholm's *Deadliest Enemy: Our War Against Killer Germs*

Peggy Orenstein's *Girls & Sex: Navigating the Complicated New Landscape*

Thomas Paine's *Common Sense*

William Penn's *Some Fruits of Solitude* (editor, Eric Taylor)

Robert Putnam's *Our Kids: The American Dream in Crisis*

Michael Sandel's *Justice: What's the Right Thing to Do*

Ben Sasse's *The Vanishing American Adult: Our Coming-of-Age Crisis—and How to Rebuild a Culture of Self-Reliance*

David Sheff's *Clean: Overcoming Addiction and Ending America's Greatest Tragedy*

Matthew Skinta and Aisling Curtin's *Mindfulness and Acceptance for Gender and Sexual Minorities*

Joseph Stiglitz's *The Price of Inequality: How Today's Divided Society Endangers Our Future*

273

274

Clif Stratton's *Education for Empire: American Schools, Race, and the Paths of Good Citizenship*

Chris Wallace's *Character: Profiles in Presidential Courage*

Tom Wong's *The Politics of Immigration: Partisanship, Demographic Change, and American National Identity*

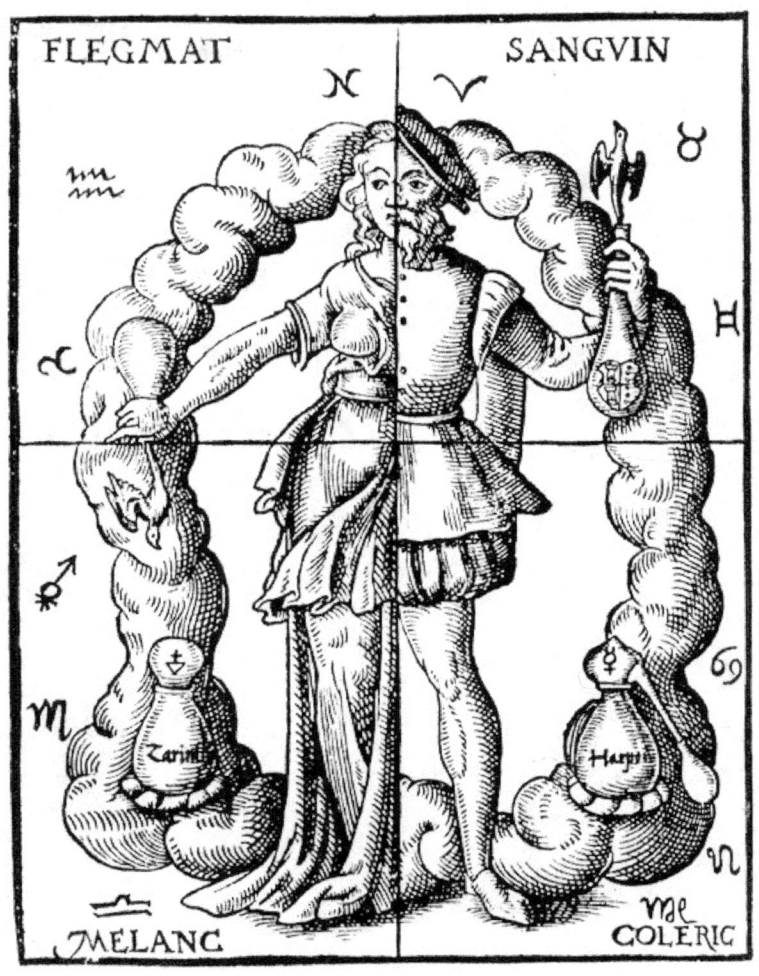

Trumplosion Illustrations

[Again, most (but not all) of the images used for illustrations in *Trumplosion* were originally color images but were converted to black and white images for cost considerations.]

Cover, Sunday Record-Herald, "Lady Liberty and Liberty Bell," New York
      Public Library, Public Domain collection
Trumplosion Image, ParentRap, Pixabay image
Colton's Map of North America, New York Public Library, Public Domain
      collection
The Seal of the United States of America, Wikimedia Commons image
JFK Stamp, Wikimedia Commons image
FDR, Four Freedoms Stamp, Wikimedia Commons image
"Truth Matters," Mark Dixon, Wikimedia Commons image, cropped
"Lack of Empathy Is Dangerous," Mark Dixon, Wikimedia Commons image,
      cropped
"Charity" by Hans Sebal Beham, New York Public Library, Public Domain
      collection
"Justice" by Hans Sebal Beham, New York Public Library, Public Domain
      collection
"He Is Not Above the Law," Elvert Barnes, Wikimedia Commons image,
      cropped
Trump holding the decapitated head of the Statue of Liberty, Wikimedia
      Commons image, cropped
Public Domain Patriotic Label (Pre-Election) (Poetry)
"Peace for all Nations" Flag, New York Public Library, Public Domain
      collection
"Nations United for Victory" Stamp, Wikimedia Commons image
Blind Justice with cherubim, New York Public Library, Public Domain
      collection
"The Constitution/Our Union Forever," New York Public Library, Public
      Domain collection
Red Lincoln Stamp, Wikimedia Commons image
Trump groping the Statue of Liberty, Elvert Barnes, Wikimedia Commons
      image, cropped
Red Female Symbol with Fist, Sam, Wikimedia Commons image, cropped
"America and Old Glory," New York Public Library, Public Domain collection
"Statue of Liberty by Night," New York Public Library, Public Domain
      collection
Public Domain Patriotic Label (Post-Election) (Poetry)

Eagle biting Snake and stepping on Cactus, New York Public Library, Public
    Domain collection
Trump as Putin's Puppet, Elvert Barnes, Wikimedia Commons image, cropped
Blue Independence Hall, New York Public Library, Public Domain image
"I'm with Her [Earth image]," photograph by author
International Cooperation Year Stamp, Wikimedia Commons image
"The Constitution Follows the Flag," New York Public Library, Public Domain
    collection
Trump Image and Word Collage, johnhain, Pixabay Image
Flag and Emblem Gold Eagle, New York Public Library, Public Domain
    collection
"Those who Deny freedom to others Deserve it not for Themselves" Stamp,
    Flickr's "Public Domain—Stamps" image
Susan B Anthony Stamp, Flickr's "Public Domain—Stamps" image
Bald Eagle at nest with eaglets, Wikimedia Commons image
"E Pluribus Unum" Eagle with shield and flag, New York Public Library, Public
    Domain collection
"My Country's Flag," New York Public Library, Public Domain collection
"Our Republic and its Press Will or Fall Together" Stamp, Wikimedia
    Commons image
"America's Light Fueled by Truth and Reason" Stamp, Wikimedia Commons
    image
Seal of the President of the United States, Wikimedia Commons image
American Eagle image, New York Public Library, Public Domain collection
"I have Sworn ... Hostility against every form of Tyranny over the mind of
    man" Stamp, Flickr's "Public Domain—Stamps" image
Quartet of "A Root of Democracy" Stamps, Wikimedia Commons image
"Keep Your Policies Off My Body," ze wrestler, Wikimedia Commons image,
    cropped
"Family Planning" Stamp, Wikimedia Commons image
"I'M With the Resistance," Mark Dixon, Wikimedia Commons image
"Shed Walls, Don't Build Them," Mark Dixon, Wikimedia Commons image
Sunday Record-Herald, "Lady Liberty with Liberty Bell," New York Public
    Library, Public Domain collection
"Rosie the Riveter," National Archives' Powers of Persuasion: Posters from
    World War II collection
Children celebrating Washington's Birthday, New York Public Library, Public
    Domain collection
Children's Stamp, Wikimedia Commons image
Photograph of two eaglets, Wikimedia Commons image
"Saluting Young America" Stamp, Wikimedia Commons image
"Truth May Be Kept Down, but Not Crushed," New York Public Library, Public
    Domain collection
"Impeach the Constitution-Breaking Psychopathic Liar!" photograph by the
    author

"Save the Earth, Literally Everything Depends Upon It," photograph by the author

"Unless Someone Like You Cares a Whole Awful Lot, Nothing Is Going to Change. It's Not." photograph by the author

"Save the Planet, Don't Screw It, Pruitt," photograph by the author

"There's No Planet B," photograph by the author

National Parks Centennial Stamp, Wikimedia Commons image

"Reality Strikes, Science, Climate Change Now," photograph by the author

Gardening/Horticulture Stamp, Flickr's "Public Domain—Stamps" image

"Greed and Stupidity Are Killing Our Planet," photograph by the author

"There Are No Jobs on a Dead Planet," photograph by the author

Yellowstone Stamp, Wikimedia Commons image

"Green not Greed," photograph by the author

"Keep It Clean Enough to Eat Off Of," photograph by the author

"Save Time, Impeach Now," Mark Dixon, Wikimedia Commons image, cropped

"#45, Mockery Worldwide," Elvert Barnes, Wikimedia Commons image, cropped

Blue Lincoln Stamp, Flickr's "Public Domain—Stamps" image

"Rule or Ruin," cropped image of "Shall the people rule. W.J. Bryan" (1908), Library of Congress image

Eagle and Flags, New York Public Library, Public Domain collection

Public Domain Patriotic Label (Post-Election) (Essays)

Statue of Liberty at Dawn, New York Public Library, Public Domain collection

Photograph of John Lewis, Wikimedia Commons image

"A Public That Reads/A Root of Democracy" Stamp, Wikimedia Commons image

Photograph of Lyndon Johnson and Civil Rights Leaders, Wikimedia Commons image

Columbia Wearing a New Costume of Freedom after the Freeing of the Slaves, New York Public Library, Public Domain collection

"300th Anniversary of Printing in Colonial America" Stamp, Wikimedia Commons image

"Independence Hall" Stamp, Wikimedia Commons image

"Rise of the Spirit of Independence" Stamp, Wikimedia Commons image

"Freedom of the Press" Stamp, Wikimedia Commons image

Justice Stamp, New York Public Library, Public Domain collection

"Make America Think Again!/Science is Real," ze wrestler, Wikimedia Commons image, cropped

"Idiocracy was just supposed to be a Movie, not a Documentary," Mark Dixon, Wikimedia Commons, cropped

Statue of Liberty Word Collage, johnhain, Pixabay image

Columbia, Columbus, Map of US, and Eagle, New York Public Library, Public Domain collection

Patriotic Image of George Washington, New York Public Library, Public Domain collection

"An Orange Monarch I Support," photograph by the author
The Signing of the Declaration of Independence, New York Public Library,
Public Domain collection
"Diagram of the Federal Government," New York Public Library, Public
Domain collection
Thomas Paine, New York Public Library, Public Domain collection
Common Sense, New York Public Library, Public Domain collection
Alexander Hamilton Stamp, Wikimedia Commons image
George Washington Stamp, Wikimedia Commons image
Thomas Jefferson, New York Public Library, Public Domain collection
"The Journal of American History," New York Public Library, Public Domain
collection
"The Mirror of the Whole of Nature and the Image of Art," Robert Fludd's
Great Chain of Being, "R. Fludd, Utriusque cosmi maioris scilicet,"
Wikimedia Commons/Wellcome Images image
Ernst Haeckel's Diagram of the Races of Men and Apes, (1870)
(http://archive.org/details/natrlichesch1868haec), Internet Archive
image
"The Mongolian [Chinese] Octopus," Phillip May, (1886) Wikimedia Commons
image
"History Repeats Itself" by Watson Heston, (1896) "antisemetic political
cartoon in Sound Money." Wikimedia Commons image
"The Destructive Mormon Monster," Frederick Opper, (1884) Wikimedia
Commons image
"The Papal Octopus," (1913) Wikimedia Commons image
Image from Remmelin's Anatomical Flap Book (1667), *The Public Domain
Review*, "Remmelin's Anatomical 'Flap' Book (1667)"
"Keep Abortion Legal," Wikimedia Commons image, cropped
"Keep Abortion Safe and Legal," Wikimedia Commons image, cropped
"Americans All, Immigrants All," (1938-39) U.S. Department of the Interior,
Office of Education, poster for radio broadcast series.
"Save the Earth, It's the Only Planet with Wine," photograph by the author
"To Thine Own Self Be True," Thomas Nast, 1875, New York Public Library,
Public Domain collection
"The Union as It Was," Thomas Nast, 1874, New York Public Library, Public
Domain collection
"Shall We Call Home Our Troops?" Charles Stanley Reinhart, 1875, New
York Public Library, Public Domain collection
"Of Course He Wants to Vote the Democratic Ticket," Arthur Burdett Frost,
1876, Wikimedia Commons
"Hula Dancers," John B. Wilson, Midway, World's Columbia Exhibition, 1893,
Wikimedia Commons
"It's a Small World—India," Disney World, Kirsten5300, Wikimedia Commons
Public Domain Patriotic Label (Post-Election) (Short Stories)
"Oceans Are Rising and So Are We!" photograph by the author

Uncle Sam "Brothers in Arms," New York Public Library, Public Domain
        collection
"You Can't Eat [image of dollar bills]," photograph by the author
"Love Your Mother" and an image of earth, photograph by the author
Justice with Flags Stamp, Wikimedia Commons image
Blue American Eagle Stamp, Wikimedia Commons image
"No Mines Near Sacred Sites," photograph by the author
"Search for Peace" Stamp, Wikimedia Commons image
Map of North America, New York Public Library, Public Domain collection
"American Bald Eagle Stamp, Wikimedia Commons image
"One Planet, One Chance, Honor the Paris Agreement," photograph by the
        author
Melpomene and Thalia, New York Public Library, Public Domain collection
"Service Above Self" Stamp, Wikimedia Commons image
"Collective Bargaining" Stamp, Wikimedia Commons image
Princess Map of North and South America, New York Public Library, Public
        Domain collection
American Suspender image, New York Public Library, Public Domain
        collection
FDR Four Freedoms Stamp, Wikimedia Commons image
"To the Fine Arts" Stamp, Wikimedia Commons image
The Liberty Bell, New York Public Library, Public Domain collection
Green Four Freedoms Stamp, Wikimedia Commons image
"E Pluribus Unum" Eagle with shield and flag, New York Public Library, Public
        Domain collection
Compound Microscope, Wikimedia Commons image
"No Drilling in National Parks," photograph by the author
"This Druid Loves Gaia," photograph by the author
"Climate Change is Real," photograph by the author
"Clean Energy Saves Lives!" photograph by the author
Columbia, New York Public Library, Public Domain collection
"As a Lute Out of Tune," from Robert Burton's *The Anatomy of Melancholy*
        (1621), The Public Domain Review, "As a Lute out of Tune: Robert
        Burton's Melancholy"
"A Woman's Place is in the Resistance," Pixabay image
Backcover, Trumplosion Image, ParentRap, Pixabay image

www.ingramcontent.com/pod-product-compliance
Lightning Source LLC
Chambersburg PA
CBHW070311260626
47160CB00003B/806